Strength in Weakness

Langham

PREACHING RESOURCES

Written in small and accessible portions, this book is full of vitamin shots of God's grace, shaping our understanding of the reality of the Christian life and life in community. It opens our eyes to what it means to live within our own Christian communities, and to be aware of what God wants to do through a group of people who are weak and complex, yet who are strong in him.

Carmen Castillo
Sub-regional Coordinator,
Southern Cone, IFES Latin America

In a very clear and faithful manner, without avoiding the scholarly debates, Jonathan Lamb opens the book of 2 Corinthians with such skillfulness and simplicity that its message comes alive today, stirring the mind, gripping the heart, and challenging the reader to godly living and authentic biblical ministry in an age of showmanship. This is a great tool for pastoral and preaching ministry.

Emeka Egbo
Associate Director for Africa, Langham Preaching

Every leader must be a person of integrity in all their relationships, so that those whom they lead will be able to trust their words and actions. Maintaining integrity is often demanding, yet by God's grace we are able to find strength in our weakness. I highly recommend this book by Jonathan Lamb, which addresses the challenge of upholding integrity and shows us how we can find strength in weakness through Christ.

Rev Dr Patrick Fung
General Director, OMF International

In God's kindness, the wonderful letter of 2 Corinthians is in our Bibles to give us detailed insight into the true nature of authentic Christian ministry. It is a very encouraging and challenging letter that will greatly benefit the preacher and the congregation if its message is clearly heard and then faithfully preached. However, 2 Corinthians is also a demanding letter, and this is why this introduction to 2 Corinthians is so very helpful. To teach things simply you need to understand them profoundly, and that is certainly the case when it comes to the writing of this volume. With incisive observation, pastoral wisdom and careful attention to the original context, this will be a terrific help to you as you wrestle with this tear-stained letter. I warmly commend this book and assure you that with Jonathan's help your understanding of this letter, your dependence on God in ministry, and your own heart will each be greatly enlarged. As you study 2 Corinthians may you find awesome strength in God as he works faithfully through your own weakness.

Jonathan Gemmell
Director of Conferences and Resources,
The Proclamation Trust

As a weekly preacher I am looking for a commentary that explains the text clearly, provides warm, realistic, accurate and challenging application, is written by someone with real ministry experience, keeps a strong focus on the gospel, and stirs my own heart as I prepare with God's help to stir others. For these reasons, Jonathan Lamb's commentary will be my "go to" resource for 2 Corinthians. The headings themselves are sermon outlines in waiting.

Jeremy McQuoid, DMin
Teaching Pastor,
Deeside Christian Fellowship Church, Aberdeen, UK
Chairman of Trustees, Keswick Ministries

As someone who has been involved in the ministry of Bible teaching, I thank God for this outstanding Bible study. Jonathan Lamb's book is a useful contribution and the choice of 2 Corinthians is brilliant. The style is easy to follow and useful for all those who want to study, practice and teach. I am impressed by the balance between content and purpose. Lamb brings his rich experience and personal study into this refreshing treatment of Paul's very personal epistle. I strongly endorse this book – it should be on the desk of any serious Bible student or teacher of the word.

CB Samuel
Theological Advisor, Micah Global
and the Evangelical Fellowship of India Commission on Relief

Strength in Weakness

An Introduction to 2 Corinthians

Jonathan Lamb

Langham
PREACHING RESOURCES

Revised text © 2020 Jonathan Lamb

Published 2020 by Langham Preaching Resources
An imprint of Langham Publishing
www.langhampublishing.org

Originally published in 1999 by Crossway Books, Leicester, England, as
2 Corinthians: Crossway Bible Guide

Langham Publishing and its imprints are a ministry of Langham Partnership

Langham Partnership
PO Box 296, Carlisle, Cumbria, CA3 9WZ, UK
www.langham.org

ISBNs:
978-1-83973-041-2 Print
978-1-83973-042-9 ePub
978-1-83973-043-6 Mobi
978-1-83973-044-3 PDF

British Library Cataloguing-in-Publication Data
A catalogue record for this book is available from the British Library

ISBN: 978-1-83973-041-2

Cover & Book Design: projectluz.com

Dedicated to the memory of George Lamb and Ben Taylor, who lived humble yet fruitful lives in dependence on God's strength in the midst of weakness.

Contents

Section 3: Paul Appeals for Generosity – 2 Corinthians 8:1–9:15

Section 4: Paul Exerts His Authority – 2 Corinthians 10:1–13:14

Welcome!

Using This Book

There are three important features of this book which will help you to understand and apply the message of 2 Corinthians.

First, our purpose is to provide a clear introductory commentary on the text. We have broken up the text into distinct units and have also used simple headings to help summarise the meaning of the passage. There is not much space for illustration and application, but we hope that the clear explanation of the text will allow readers, small groups and preachers to then work hard at how best to apply the passages. It will be important to read the sections of this book with your Bible open at the relevant passage, since we have not reproduced the full Bible text in each section.

Second, there are "boxes" of extra comments throughout the commentary to give important additional background information which will help with both understanding and explaining the passages. Some give additional background material that will help readers to understand the context, and some relate to passages which have important doctrines contained within them. We hope this will be useful additional information as we think about how to explain the passages to others.

Third, at the end of each section there are a few questions which can be used for personal reflection or for group discussion.

Using This Book for Personal Study

It would be good to begin by praying and reading through the specific passage and its associated commentary a number of times, before looking at the questions. You may find it helpful to note down your answers to the questions, along with any other thoughts you may have. Putting pen to paper will help you think through the issues and how they specifically apply to your own situation. It will also be encouraging to look back over all that God has been teaching you. Talk about what you are learning with a friend. Pray together that you will be able to apply all these new lessons to your life.

Using This Book in a Small Group: A Note to Group Leaders

In preparation for the study, please pray and read the specific passage of Scripture and its associated commentary a number of times. Use other resource material such as a Bible dictionary if these are available in your country.

At the top of each chapter we have stated the broad theme; this is the core truth you want your group to take away with them. With this in mind, decide which questions you should spend the most time on, and add questions that would be helpful to your group or particular church situation. Before people come, encourage them to read the passage you will be studying (and also the relevant section of this commentary, if they have a copy of the book).

Make sure you leave time at the end of the study for people to apply what they are learning to their own situation and to pray together.

Preaching from 2 Corinthians

Just a note for preachers. This title is published by Langham Preaching Resources, and there are Langham Preaching movements now established in many parts of the world. Many readers might be members of small preaching clubs or fellowship groups, and perhaps you can work together on the questions to be found after each section of this book. Most importantly, we encourage preachers to focus on three issues:

1. *Am I being faithful* to the Bible passage? – Am I reflecting the meaning of the passage, so that I truly express what the original writer intended his original hearers to understand?

2. *Am I being clear?* – Is the way I present the preached message structured in a way which helps the listener or reader truly understand the force and flow of the passage?

3. *Am I being relevant?* – Am I making the connections with the lives of my hearers, demonstrating how the Bible passage applies to the challenges of their personal, family and church lives, as well as the mood and worldview of their culture?

These are three good questions for anyone seeking to explain the Bible passage, whether in preaching, in small groups, or in one-to-one explanation of the passage to others, and my hope is that these points are modelled in this study guide.

This book comes with all good wishes as you explore this wonderful New Testament letter! May you discover the Lord saying to you what he also said to Paul: "My grace is sufficient for you, for my power is made perfect in weakness" (2 Cor 12:9).

Jonathan Lamb
Oxford, UK

Paul and the Corinthians

Sometimes I meet people who imagine that working full time in Christian ministry must be the closest thing to heaven on this side of eternity. Spending all that time with other Christians! But anyone working in a church or Christian organization knows there is another side to the story. Christian ministry can be extremely demanding, for the church is a human as well as a divine institution. "We are God's building project," as Paul implies in 1 Corinthians 3:9, and because the building is not yet complete there are plenty of rough edges.

Paul didn't have an easy time with the Corinthians. This was partly to do with some of their internal problems, and partly to do with a fairly turbulent relationship with them. In 2 Corinthians Paul bares his soul, describing the struggles of his own ministry and the pain he feels at being criticized and misunderstood.

Part of the background to the uneasy relationship is to do with the arrival in Corinth of some false teachers. There are a number of theories about who these intruders might have been, but we will find reference being made to them and to their style of ministry throughout Paul's writing. As the letter progresses, we discover much about his critics simply by seeing how Paul defends himself. Unlike Paul, they carried special letters of commendation, they accepted financial support from the Corinthians, and they were keen on eloquent speech and erudite knowledge. They were proud of outward displays of their spirituality and wonder-working power.

Paul was clearly distressed that the Corinthians were being swayed by such teachers, accepting their false values and emphases. He even refers to these "super-apostles" as preaching "a different gospel" (11:4–5). It hurt him deeply that, in turn, the Corinthian believers whom he had brought to faith were now rejecting him, their spiritual father.

Much of his correspondence hinges around this issue – not just the attack on his integrity but the introduction of a different Jesus and a different gospel. Paul describes the nature of Christian ministry but links it clearly with the nature of the Christian gospel. How was God's power seen in the gospel? In the weakness of the crucified Jesus. In just the same way, God's power would be seen in Paul precisely through the weaknesses about which he writes so candidly.

The letter not only exposes Paul's inner feelings, but also provides us with a clear apologetic for true Christian ministry and open Christian relationships which has proved to be of abiding value to churches in every culture and every age. It represents one of the most profound descriptions of authentic Christian service ever written. It provides us with the key resources we need in order to be "strong in weakness."

Section 1

Paul Explains His Actions

2 Corinthians 1:1–2:11

1

Christian Relationships
2 Corinthians 1:1–2

Paul's opening greeting underlines the significance of our relationship with God and with fellow Christians.

Most of us know the "Christian" wording for concluding our letters – "Every blessing!" . . . "Christian greetings!" . . . "Love and prayers!" It is easy to reproduce them without giving too much thought to their meaning. Paul, in common with writers of his day, began his letters with a customary greeting and "signature," but this was no mere formality. Each phrase is pregnant with meaning, leading us into themes which the rest of the letter will explore more fully.

The opening verse uses four terms to describe important relationships in the Christian family. They introduce the themes of authority and intimacy, which we will find intermingled throughout Paul's very personal letter. He begins with his own calling.

1. An Apostle of Christ Jesus by the Will of God (1:1)

Paul is responding to a personal attack by false teachers in Corinth who questioned his authority. So he begins with a deliberate reminder that his calling as an apostle comes from God himself. This sets the tone for the whole letter. If he has been called and appointed by God, then his message has authority. It is not a matter of Paul's innate ability, but arises from the apostleship with which he has been entrusted. It is God's will (1:1) that he should serve the churches in this way.

We must come to Paul's letter recognizing that it is God's word through his specially commissioned agent. While we need to work hard to understand how it applies in our own circumstances, we cannot ignore the abiding truth which it contains. As Paul was to say to the Thessalonians, he rejoiced that they received his message not as the word of men, "but as it actually is, the word of God, which is indeed at work in you who believe" (1 Thess 2:13). Paul's message to us in 2 Corinthians has authority and life-changing power because he is an "apostle . . . by the will of God" (2 Cor 1:1).

2. Timothy Our Brother (1:1)

Timothy was with Paul when he wrote the letter, and they had an especially close relationship. Timothy had been converted through Paul's witness, and now they were fellow workers and brothers in God's family. Whenever we use the term "brother" or "sister" in Christian fellowship, we are reminding each other of the privilege of being incorporated into the church family. Here Paul actually uses the term "the brother"; perhaps it was a more formal way of describing Timothy's official role as Paul's envoy to the church in Corinth.

3. The Church of God in Corinth (1:1)

The group of believers to whom Paul writes is not called "the church in Corinth," nor are they named after Paul the apostle. The important thing is that they belong to God. However small a group of Christians might be, they have the dignity of being called "the church of God." Paul doesn't use the term to describe a building, but rather a gathering of God's specially chosen people. The word "church" describes both what we do, as those who meet together, and who we are, as those who belong to God.

4. With All the Saints throughout Achaia (1:1)

Achaia was a large Roman province to the south of Macedonia. Christians were probably scattered across the area, but nevertheless Paul identifies them as part of God's church. (It is possible that 2 Corinthians was a widely read circular letter, as 9:2 and 11:10 imply.) Paul describes the believers as "saints." This means they are God's "holy ones." It is a word used to describe all true believers, not an elite or select group of Christians. It has much more to do with living as a Christian through the rough and tumble of everyday life than it does with a figure in a stained-glass window. It is godliness in working clothes.

The Corinthian Christians lived in an age like our own, which was characterized by individualism. Self-sufficiency and self-fulfilment were not just matters for philosophical debate but were common features of everyday life. So Paul's reminder of their corporate solidarity – "the church of God that is at Corinth, with all the saints" (1:1 ESV) – would have been very important for them. It is a theme he will reinforce later in the first chapter, as well as throughout his writing. For example, the word "saint" appears many times in the New Testament, almost always in the plural. The only occasion when it occurs in the singular is in a community context: "greet every saint" (Phil 4:21 ESV).

Christians belong together. We are God's people and, wherever we may be in the world and however small or large the congregation to which we belong, God calls us to express that solidarity and community with other Christians in the most practical ways.

5. Spiritual Blessings (1:2)

Although verse 2 is a typical Pauline greeting (it appears in all of his letters except 1 and 2 Thessalonians), it is especially relevant to this letter. In the next section he will introduce us to one of his main themes: his experience of trial. All of us who are called to Christian service are sure to face pressure, but 2 Corinthians specially demonstrates that God's grace is promised to everyone undergoing trial or experiencing weakness.

"Grace and peace to you" expresses Paul's constant desire for the churches in his care. He longs that they will be enriched by these essential spiritual blessings. "Grace" expresses the fact that God is constantly giving to us, not because of what we have achieved, but because of his active love through Christ. Everything we receive comes from God's hand, whether our being forgiven and accepted in his presence, or our experience of his help in times of pressure, or the provision of our day-to-day needs. Paul was to discover that this grace would be more than sufficient, even in the toughest moments of his life (12:9). No wonder that grace has the first and last word in this very personal letter (1:2 and 13:14), for it summed up Paul's total experience of living with God.

The word "peace" embodies the same richness. It expresses the total well-being and wholeness that come to us through faith in Christ, the harmony and security of our life with God.

When we face difficulties in our lives, here are two words to hold on to. They represent the heart of the Christian message and stand for God's promise that all we need is available through our friendship with him. Paul deliberately underscores the fact that such resources are provided by "God our Father and the Lord Jesus Christ" (1:2): there is nowhere else to go to find such overwhelming richness.

Questions

1. How do you respond to this statement "The Bible is the word of God"? What authority and power does it have for us today? Discuss examples which come to mind.

2. We often refer to fellow Christians as sisters and brothers, but in what ways can we strengthen a genuine sense of "family" in our church?

3. How can "grace and peace" become an everyday experience for us? To what extent does the outside world see grace and peace in us?

2

Comfort in Suffering
2 Corinthians 1:3–7

Suffering provides the opportunity for experiencing
God's comfort and for sharing that comfort with others.

We will see that the opening themes of chapter 1 are suffering and comfort, and these are the key to understanding the whole of Paul's letter. In common with many of his letters, the opening thanksgiving represents a trailer or preview for the main feature film which is to follow.

Paul was under attack by some in Corinth who doubted that he was a genuine apostle, and already in verse 1 he has stressed that his calling is from God. We will encounter Paul's defence against these various accusations throughout the letter, but in this section he defends the integrity of his ministry as an apostle by showing that suffering is part of authentic Christian ministry. More than that, such suffering is the very occasion when God's comforting grace can be experienced. Knowing God's help when under pressure provokes Paul's thanksgiving in verse 3. In this section he shows how suffering is related to three important themes.

1. Suffering and God's Comfort (1:3–4)

The ability to praise God in the midst of pressure can come only from an experience of God's strengthening comfort. The key word "comfort" is found ten times in five verses, and the same idea is found throughout the letter ("comfort" or "encourage" is used in 2:7; 7:4, 6, 7, 13; and 8:4, 6, 17, along with many references to "urge" or "appeal"). No one translation will do justice to the various contexts: some Bibles translate the word as "comfort," some as "encouragement" and some as "consolation."

The same word is used in the name given to the Holy Spirit in John's Gospel (John 14:16, 26; 15:26; 16:7). The Spirit's ministry of help and encouragement, drawing alongside to strengthen us when we are tested, is the essence of what Paul describes in this section (2 Cor 1:3–7). Paul is deeply thankful that God is standing with him during these moments of suffering, and this is the testimony of God's people throughout history. As David sang in Psalm 23, "Even though I walk through the darkest valley, I will fear no evil, for you are with me" (v. 4).

Paul refers to the source of that comfort in three phrases in verse 3. Just as grace and peace come from "God our Father and the Lord Jesus Christ" (v. 2), so our comfort comes from the "Father of our Lord Jesus Christ, the Father of compassion and the God of all comfort." These expressions show that Paul believes in a God who cares. They are not simply technical or religious phrases. There is a profound intimacy in Paul's description of God our Father. It is true for all Christians: we often come to know our Father best through suffering.

2. Suffering and Christ's Ministry (1:5)

The other important words in this section are translated "trouble" or "suffering," and they are used frequently in this letter. The first word means pressure of various kinds. One form of ancient torture was to place a large boulder on a person's chest, a crushing pressure that would squeeze the life out of them. The second word usually describes suffering inflicted upon us by others.

Christians are to expect pressure in their lives. It is the rule rather than the exception. In fact, Jesus promised us as much (John 16:33). But why should suffering be a natural and normal part of life for Christians? Paul explains that suffering is the inevitable result of being united to Christ: "the sufferings of Christ flow over into our lives" (2 Cor 1:5). Paul will reinforce the idea later in the letter (4:10–12; 13:4). His experience of trouble and affliction flows from belonging to Christ and sharing in Christ's ministry.

Far from being evidence of Paul's lack of spirituality, or casting doubt on the genuineness of his apostleship, suffering was a badge of his discipleship, a clear indication that he was fulfilling his God-given ministry in serving Christ.

This verse certainly does not imply that Christ's suffering in securing our redemption needs extending or completing through the experience of Christians. His suffering was unique, complete, once and for all, as Paul explains in his letter to the Romans (Rom 6:10). Rather, Paul is describing the intimate relationship between Christ and those who bear his name. Our life is his life, with its sufferings and also its eventual glory (Rom 8:17; Phil 3:10; 2 Tim 2:12; 1 Pet 4:13).

This gives Christian suffering a sense of dignity and, in his defence of his apostleship, it is no wonder that Paul "boasted" about his weaknesses. The more he suffered, the more it was evidence of his high calling to be identified with Christ. The same argument of solidarity with Christ appears in the second part of verse 5. If we are united with Christ in his suffering, we will also experience the abundance of God's comfort overflowing in our lives through Christ. The connection is made with the phrase "just as" (2 Cor 1:5). No matter what pressure or affliction we might suffer as Christians, this is more than matched by God's strengthening presence (4:16–17; 12:9).

3. Suffering and Christian Community (1:4, 6–7)

If we are united to Christ, we are therefore united to one another. Christians are bound to Christ and bound to every other believer. There is a community dimension to Christian experience, including our experience of suffering and comfort.

We might not all be called to be Bible teachers, and we might not have dramatic gifts of healing. But if we know Christ, we will have a vital ministry to exercise, described in verses 4 and 6. Paul presents us with a sequence. First, we will experience the overflow of Christ's sufferings. Then we will know the strengthening of his comfort; and precisely because of this experience, we will have the ministry of comforting others: "so that we can comfort those in any trouble with the comfort we ourselves receive from God" (1:4). As we experience the Lord standing alongside us in times of pressure, so we become qualified to bring encouragement and help to others. It is this which brings a quality of tenderness to all true Christian ministry.

We might not experience the same pressures or troubles as others, but that does not limit our ministry. The experience of comfort itself is the basis for helping others. We are able to help one another "in any trouble" (v. 4). Paul was able to say that his own experience of suffering would prove to be a benefit to the Corinthian believers (v. 6), as he repeats later in the letter (4:5, 15).

The community emphasis of suffering and comfort is further emphasized by Paul's use of "share" in verse 7, the word for fellowship and partnership. Paul is absolutely certain that the Corinthians will experience divine comfort which will sustain them in their difficulties. He describes his hope for them as "firm," a commercial term meaning giltedged, secure and reliable. The God of all comfort has not failed him, and neither will God fail the Corinthians.

When passing through difficulties it is never easy to have the presence of mind to assess objectively how God has helped us. But it is good to remember when the pressure is on that God redeems those moments, using them for his good purposes of strengthening others in the Christian family.

Questions

1. Can you recall times when you have experienced God's comfort when under pressure? Share your experiences with others to help them.

2. We have seen in this passage that our lives are linked to Jesus's life, involving both suffering and glory. Read through the verses mentioned (Rom 8:17; Phil 3:10; 2 Tim 2:12; 1 Pet 4:13) and turn them into prayer and thanksgiving.

3. If you could see your life as essentially being one with Christ, what difference would that make to the way you live?

4. The world in general sees suffering purely as an evil to be eliminated, or at least avoided. How can we help people to see that there might be positive value in suffering?

Health and Wealth

One of the primary lessons of 2 Corinthians is that the Christian faith offers no immunity from suffering. Throughout the letter Paul demonstrates that there is a vital connection between the gospel and the Christian life. God's power was seen in the weakness of the crucified Jesus, and, since being a Christian is to be united to Christ, God's power is seen best in weak people.

Success-oriented spirituality, which suggests that Christians should be immune to difficulty, is a distortion of the Christian message. The kind of Christian teaching which implies that, if only we had enough faith, we could avoid the pressures of sickness, or unemployment, or poverty, or inner turmoil, is not only cruel to those who are passing through difficulty, but a denial of the heart of the gospel message. For Jesus walked the pathway of suffering, and there is no escaping such pressure if we are going to stand up for him in today's world. Learning to see this as part of the privilege of being identified with Jesus will help us to view our sufferings from the proper perspective.

In some Christian circles an emphasis is placed on so-called "prosperity theology," which suggests that it is not God's will for us to be poor or unhealthy. But there are fundamental weaknesses with such a position.

1. A Wrong Handling of the Bible

In prosperity teaching many Bible texts are lifted out of their context and interpreted incorrectly as a result. Promises made by God to his people under the old covenant are applied to Christians today without proper thought given to the original context. For example, in Galatians, Paul uses the phrase the "blessing of Abraham," but it would be a mistake to interpret this as the blessings listed in Deuteronomy 28:1–14 (prosperity, health, fertility, victory in battle). Paul is writing about new covenant blessings, and so the blessing of Abraham is a synonym for forgiveness and peace with God, as he describes it in Galatians 3 and Romans 4.

Similarly, it would be a mistake to interpret Isaiah 53:5, "by his wounds we are healed," to imply that, as a result of Christ's work, every believer should be healed of every infirmity in this life. It needs to be understood in the light of the rest of the Bible's teaching, where it is clear that the full benefits of Christ's work will be seen only when Christ returns, and the kingdom is fully realized.

Equally, words are misunderstood because of the failure to interpret them in their setting. To take an example from 2 Corinthians, what did Paul mean when he said that Christ became poor, "so that you through his poverty might become rich" (2 Cor 8:9)? Is that a promise of financial blessing? Once we study the passage in context, we realize the meaning of the word "rich" is related to the meaning of Christ's riches before he came into this world at Bethlehem. Because he laid aside his rights, and suffered death on the cross, we now inherit all of the heavenly blessings which belong to him.

2. A Wrong Perspective on the Kingdom

Think for a moment about healing. All of us would want to affirm God's ability to intervene and heal the sick; none of us should ever be cynical about that possibility. But the biblical teaching on this theme is related to what is referred to as "the now and the not yet." Paul's use of the idea of firstfruits is a helpful illustration of what we are to expect (e.g. Rom 8:23). If God's kingdom is here, we should expect to see signs of the kingdom now; there should be some evidence of his powerful working – what we might call the "firstfruits." We rejoice with those who are healed, whether through the care of doctors or through the exercise of a healing gift within the Christian community.

But there is also a "not yet." The full experience of what it means to live in God's kingdom, with all of its wholeness, peace and restoration, is yet to come. We still live our lives within the overlap of this present age and the age to come. So the book of Revelation anticipates the day when this present age is finished: "'He will wipe away every tear from their eyes. There will be no more death' or mourning or crying or pain; for the old order of things has passed away" (Rev 21:4).

So it is wise to avoid both errors: both the error of suggesting that there is no fruit on the tree, and the error (of prosperity theology) of suggesting that the tree must be full of fruit now. The biblical concept of firstfruits is realistic: we expect some evidence of God's intervention, and we pray for it in humble dependence on his wisdom and sovereignty. But we should not expect everything to be resolved now.

3. A Wrong Understanding of Prayer

The lesson of Paul's experience, described in 2 Corinthians 12, is that God is not duty bound to give us everything we ask for, as if prayer were some kind of New Age magic for getting whatever you want. In a wise comment on James 5:15, Alec Motyer rightly points out that if God had to give us everything we asked for, we would soon stop praying. We would not have sufficient confidence in our own wisdom. It would place a terrible burden on us, for how can we anticipate what is best for us or our family, or what tomorrow's circumstances will look like?

As Motyer points out, to pray "Your will be done" does not impose a restriction on our praying, but instead it lifts the limitations of our own human knowledge. The prayer of faith is the prayer which rests in the certainty of a gracious Father giving what is best for his children.[1]

Paul came to realize that, while he did not receive the relief for which he was praying, he received something immeasurably greater: the Lord said to him, "My grace is sufficient for you, for my power is made perfect in weakness" (2 Cor 12:9).

---

1. Alec Motyer, *The Message of James*, The Bible Speaks Today (Leicester: IVP, 1985), 199.

3

God's Deliverance
2 Corinthians 1:8–11

> Suffering has the special benefit of
> teaching us to depend more fully on God
> rather than on our own resources.

Paul describes the hardships he had suffered in the province of Asia (verse 8), and although the details of those sufferings are not clear, their severity certainly is. It is possible that Paul is referring to his ministry in Ephesus where, as he said in his first letter, he "fought wild beasts" (1 Cor 15:32). For two years he struggled to proclaim Christ in a context of active opposition from others, whether from occult forces, from those who had a vested interest in other local deities or from mob violence (Acts 19).

On top of that, he taught publicly for many hours a day, and also carried the burden of pastoral care for many young Christians. Neither should we forget that he continued his normal employment, making tents, alongside everything else. It is also possible that Paul is referring to the impact of a recurrent illness, given the fact that verse 10 has an echo of Job 33:30, where Job's experience is seen in life and death terms. In this section of 2 Corinthians, he tells us openly both of the unbearable pressures and of the ways in which God met him.

1. God Teaches Us to Rely on Him (1:8–9)

Paul is remarkably honest in describing his experience. His language in verses 8 and 9 is striking: "under great pressure, far beyond our ability to endure, so that

we despaired of life itself. Indeed, we felt we had received the sentence of death"
(2 Cor 1:8–9). One paraphrase reads: "We were completely overwhelmed, the
burden was more than we could bear; in fact we told ourselves that this was
the end" (PHILLIPS). Paul felt as if the waves were crashing against the bows
and he was close to sinking.

These raw wounds are here for a purpose. Why was this happening to
an apostle, a man of God? Why was God allowing him to go through such
experiences of despair?

Paul explains what he had discovered in verse 9: "But this happened that we
might not rely on ourselves but on God." The purpose of walking this pathway
was to destroy in Paul any possible confidence in himself. Throughout the letter
Paul emphasizes that God takes us through these afflictions in order to bring
us to a recognition of our own helplessness, to bring our self-confidence to
an end, and to teach us an exclusive trust in God. In desperate times we learn
to hold him fast.

God's purpose in our lives is not to bypass difficulties but to transform
them. He does not magically remove us from the pressures, but instead uses
those very events to expose our complete inadequacy and demonstrate his
complete reliability. If we fail to learn these lessons, then the real tragedy of
Christian suffering is the wasted opportunity.

2. God Delivers Us as We Trust Him (1:10)

As he describes this life-threatening experience, Paul underlines that God can
be trusted as the one "who raises the dead" (1:9). Although he had written to
the Corinthians about the doctrine of the resurrection in his first letter, here he
is describing not a future hope but a daily reality. God can raise up Christians
who, like Paul, are despairing of life itself. Because God had delivered him from
"such a deadly peril," Paul knew God could be trusted for further deliverance,
now and in the future: "on him we have set our hope" (v. 10). Paul Barnett is
right to point out that God's deliverances in this life are always partial. "We
may recover from an illness, but there is no way to side-step our last enemy,
death. We are inextricably tangled in the sorrow and suffering of the world,
whose form is passing away. Only in the resurrection of the dead is there perfect
deliverance."[1] Nevertheless, in despairing moments in our lives we should learn
to trust the God of compassion and resurrection. He will not let go of his hold

---

1. Paul Barnett, *The Message of 2 Corinthians*, The Bible Speaks Today (Leicester: IVP,
1988), 34, 35.

on us. He is the one who can be trusted to deliver us now, in the future, and on the final day of resurrection (see box labelled "Resurrection," p. 73).

3. God Answers Prayer (1:11)

Paul not only acknowledges his dependence on God (1:9). He also affirms his dependence on God's people: "as you help us by your prayers" (v. 11). Once again Paul is underlining the importance of Christian community. Perhaps his main purpose in this opening section of the letter is to remind the Corinthians of the special bond of fellowship and unity he feels towards them, in spite of the difficulties of his relationship with them. God had delivered him, but that was a direct result of their prayers for him. In his letter Paul will express his deep affection for them; he longs that they too will express their support for him, not least in their prayerful solidarity with him.

Our prayers for each other achieve something in God's hands. Paul was not too proud to acknowledge that as an apostle he was in desperate need both of God's help and of the community's prayers. To pray, he implies, is to work with God in achieving his purpose – "as you help" (v. 11). And he links prayer with thanksgiving. The more prayer there is, the more God's people everywhere will join in praise at what God is achieving (v. 11). Once again, Paul sees this as part of God's "gracious favour" (v. 11).

As if to underline how important the relationship with the Corinthians is to him, Paul has used the opening verses of his letter to stress Christian fellowship: we will suffer together, we will be able to comfort each other, and we must pray for each other.

Questions

1. As you think of fellow Christians in your group or church congregation, what kinds of pressures do they face? In what ways might we be able to help them?

2. How can we be more effective in our prayerful solidarity with other believers, particularly those in other parts of the world who are under pressure?

3. In what ways are we tempted to "rely on ourselves" rather than to "hope in God"?

4

Paul's Faithfulness

2 Corinthians 1:12–22

In responding to claims that his word couldn't be trusted, Paul demonstrates the foundations of true Christian integrity.

Paul was being criticized for his apparent freedom to break promises and change plans. He was accused of vacillation, promising to visit the Corinthians and then not turning up. He was acting deviously and insincerely, his critics said; instead of being transparent he had been evasive. Paul will explain why he had changed his plans, but first he responds with clear arguments not only to explain what lay behind his behaviour and motivation, but also to introduce important certainties in the Christian life.

1. His Conscience (1:12–14)

Paul expresses a reason for boasting in 1:12, the first of many references to boasting, which might at first sight seem rather arrogant. As we will see, this is an attempt not to inflate his ego but to defend his integrity. Using the same device as his opponents, Paul boasts about his credentials – but unlike his opponents, he will boast about his weaknesses (11:30). In this chapter, his first line of defence is to stress that his conscience is clear: he has acted with sincerity in all of his actions towards the Corinthians (1:12).

This verse is a good definition of what integrity should mean: a clear and untroubled conscience before God, and an open and sincere relationship towards others. Everything is above board. Paul has acted in a direct and uncomplicated manner.

How has he been able to be so consistent? He returns again to the theme of God's grace (v. 12) to demonstrate that his behaviour was governed by godly standards and not by human wisdom.

He presses the point of integrity still further by stating that, just as he is not guilty of double standards or inconsistency in his behaviour, neither is he guilty of "mixed messages" in his writing (v. 13). He means what he says, and he says what he means. There is no attempt to conceal or to deceive. He is not like the person who once wrote a reference for an employee applying for another job: "If you knew him the way I know him you would feel about him the same way I feel about him!" Paul's behaviour and his writing are unambiguous. He has no hidden agenda. There is no need to read between the lines, for his message is straightforward and reliable.

To heighten the sense of seriousness in Paul's defence, he refers to the final day of judgment (v. 14). His conscience is clear, and on that final day they will understand that he has acted with integrity. It is a bold statement, and it demonstrates Paul's complete conviction that his life and conduct can be examined openly not only by fellow believers but by the piercing eye of the Judge of all.

2. His Motives (1:15–17)

Paul describes his travel plans in verse 16. He had hoped to visit the Corinthians both on his way to Macedonia and on his way back, and he was not taking matters lightly as he prepared his itinerary. His motives were not selfish; his travel was planned for their benefit (1:15). The word he uses here has an echo of the word for "grace." He wanted them to have a double blessing. Even his change of plans, to which he will refer more fully in the next chapter, was for their benefit.

In defending his integrity, Paul repeats the emphasis of verse 12 by underlining that he wasn't behaving "in a worldly manner" (v. 17). He wasn't saying yes and no at the same time, or making promises one day only to break them the next. His plans were prepared thoughtfully in God's presence, for the good of the Corinthian believers.

3. His Confidence (1:18–22)

In defending his own reliability, Paul uses the opportunity to explain the foundations of his own confidence in God. How can he, God's messenger, act in a way which is inconsistent with the God who sends him? He points out that God is faithful (1:18), God's Son fulfils his Father's promises (vv. 19–20), and God's Spirit has equipped Paul to be a living demonstration of God's reliability (vv. 21–22).

So concerned was he about the accusations being made against him that he dares to draw a parallel between his action and God's. "As surely as God is faithful," he stresses (v. 18). When proclaiming the gospel, he was utterly faithful both towards the Corinthians and towards God. And when describing his practical travel plans, he was being no less faithful. He wasn't a "yes and no" man, because he embodied and proclaimed the good news of Jesus Christ, the one who was always faithful in fulfilling God's promises and who always said "yes" to his Father (v. 19).

These verses underline Paul's complete confidence in the gospel of Christ. He describes Jesus Christ as "the Son of God" (v. 19); he knows God's promises have found their "fulfilment in Christ" (v. 20); and it is "in Christ" that believers are enabled to stand firm (v. 21). Defending his own reliability has led Paul to make a fundamental assertion of God's reliability. We need not fear the possibility of wavering in the faith because God can be relied upon to hold us fast in Christ. Christ himself has endorsed and fulfilled everything that God has promised.

To press the point home, Paul demonstrates that he is God's specially anointed messenger (v. 21), just like Jesus. The Corinthians shouldn't doubt his word. Indeed, all true believers are anointed for God's service in this way, for God's Spirit has been given to us to assure us that we belong to him (v. 22). Using several legal illustrations, Paul says that Christians are marked out as belonging to God (the "seal" confirmed the authenticity of a document), who has given a "deposit" to demonstrate that the contract is binding (v. 22). They are safe now and in the future.

Paul's response to the charges against him is not only to deny them vigorously but, in so doing, to demonstrate how reliable the Christian message is. For it is founded on God's faithfulness, secured through Christ's work, and guaranteed by the Spirit's presence in our lives.

Questions

1. What are the characteristics of reliability and integrity that should specially mark out a Christian today? Can you think of examples in your own context where Christian integrity is challenged, or living consistently is very difficult? How should we act, for instance, where it is "normal" to give or receive a bribe?

2. In 1:13, Paul describes how he is consistent and transparent in his communication. What might this imply for our own writing, whether in emails or on social media? What might be the balance between speaking openly, so that we are transparent, yet also speaking wisely, so that we don't injure someone?

3. Paul was quite straightforward in describing his plans but also his decision to change his plans. What important things might this tell us about guidance in the Christian life?

Paul's Travel Plans

Paul founded the church in Corinth about AD 50, during his second missionary journey. He had stayed for eighteen months and, although the church was established, it was still a relatively young and immature congregation. After Paul left, he spent over two years in Ephesus, but he kept in touch, writing a letter to the church about some specific issues of concern.

Subsequently, he received news of further serious difficulties, and wrote once again; the letter is preserved as 1 Corinthians. He hoped to follow up the letter with a personal visit, as 1 Corinthians 16 makes clear. But after sending the letter he had to change his plans. Instead of just the one visit to Corinth, he would make two – once on his way up to Macedonia and once on his way back. He would then be able to carry with him the money collected by the Corinthians for the needs of the church in Jerusalem (see box labelled "The Collection," p. 112).

But then the plan had to change once again. News arrived that the situation in Corinth wasn't good. The guidance he had given in 1 Corinthians hadn't had the desired effect. Paul decided he couldn't wait any longer, and so made an urgent visit to Corinth to try to sort out the problems. This was a most uncomfortable visit for the Corinthians, since Paul had to tackle the problems head on, and it was also an uncomfortable visit for Paul, because evidently he faced opposition within the church. This took the form of one or two people openly insulting him, the grievous offence to which Paul refers in 2 Corinthians 2:5–11. But in addition, a group of new teachers had arrived (see box labelled "Paul's Opponents," p. 43) who were also critical of Paul and had begun to influence the attitudes of the Corinthian church. No wonder Paul referred to this as a "painful visit" (2 Cor 2:1)!

After such an experience, he decided that a further visit was best avoided for the time being. The idea of the double visit was therefore dropped. Instead, Paul wrote a letter to try to address the difficulties once again, and this third letter is often referred to as the "painful" or "severe" letter (2 Cor 2:4), written with many tears (see box labelled "Paul's Letters to Corinth," p. 30).

Although Paul had the best interests of the Corinthians in mind when he changed his plans, he laid himself open to the charge of being fickle and unreliable. It was this problem which he tried to deal with in the opening two chapters of 2 Corinthians.

5

Tough Love

2 Corinthians 1:23–2:4

> **Paul's love for the Corinthians had sufficient depth and maturity for him to rebuke them when necessary.**

Within a week of arriving at the church where I would serve for seven years in pastoral ministry, a member of the fellowship gave me a word of encouragement. "God's people will break your heart," he said. A shade pessimistic, you might think, but it was realistic advice. Our responsible care for one another in the Christian community will inevitably bring with it pain as well as joy.

Paul had already been criticized by the Corinthians for being unreliable – failing to visit them when he had previously promised to do so. He now continues to explain what lay behind his actions and, as he does so, he responds to another criticism.

1. Concern and Affirmation (1:23–24)

As we saw in 1:15–17, Paul had planned to visit the Corinthians both on his way to Macedonia and also on his way back. When he last visited the church, he had the demanding task of disciplining them. He met considerable opposition, and so for both him and the Corinthians it was "a painful visit" (2:1). Rather than visit a second time he decided to write them a severe letter to encourage them to put things right. He then hoped that his next visit would be a much more joyful one.

Now he explains that his primary reason for not paying the visit they were expecting was to save them from still further pain (1:23; 2:1). He clearly loved

27

them and felt distressed both by the circumstances that caused him to write as he had done, and by the response of the Corinthians towards him. It cost him a good deal to have to rebuke them, and he wanted to avoid further pain both for him and for them.

Paul was also aware of the accusation being made against him. He was behaving, some thought, like a dictator, insensitive to the feelings of the church. But in this section, he shows that, far from being insensitive, acting with cool disregard for their feelings, the reverse was actually the case. It was precisely because of his depth of love for them that he had decided to change his plans.

Paul appeals to God as "my witness" (1:23), as he does elsewhere in his writing (1 Thess 2:5, 10). He seeks to live his life consciously in the presence of the Lord, aware of the fact that he is accountable.[1] Using such a phrase demonstrates how serious he is. But in case this should seem too heavy-handed, he grasps the opportunity to affirm the Corinthians at the same time. With characteristic pastoral wisdom he explains that he is their partner, working for their well-being. In turn, they are demonstrating a maturity of faith that is leading them towards spiritual stability (v. 24).

2. Pain and Love (2:1–4)

Having explained that he wanted to rejoice with them, not rebuke them (1:24), he reinforces the point in the opening verses of chapter 2. The purpose of his "tearful" letter was to provoke the necessary action within the Corinthian church so that, when he next visited, he would experience joy, not distress (2:2). That was the purpose of his pastoral ministry. But instead, he describes the opposite: when he wrote to them, he did so "out of great distress and anguish of heart and with many tears" (v. 4). The word for "distress" is the same as the one used in 1:4–8 which described the pressure and suffering he endured in his missionary work, hardships which brought him close to the point of death. Now he indicates that his pastoral ministry towards the Corinthians had the same characteristics: he experienced anguish of heart and many tears.

Intriguingly, he explains that his painful action towards them was "to let you know the depth of my love for you" (v. 4). The motivating force in exercising discipline was a deep concern and compassion for them.

Christian love is a realistic quality in all relationships. It isn't sentimental, ignoring wrong or sweeping difficulties under the carpet. True love is prepared

---

1. I develop this theme more fully in Jonathan Lamb, *Integrity: Leading with God Watching* (Leicester: IVP, 2006).

to confront those things which need to change, to face up to those things which are wrong, and where necessary, to rebuke those who fail. Paul demonstrates that such discipline is exercised out of love and has the person's best interests at heart. It is not a crushing criticism that enjoys watching people suffer in the process; it is a loving and firm discipline exercised towards those whom we long to see mature and grow towards what they should be. His letter was written so that the Corinthians would no longer cause him distress as a result of disorder or sin within the community, but instead would result in his rejoicing (2:3) at the way in which their fellowship was one of harmony, not discord.

All true Christian ministry brings with it the costs of exercising tough love. We have already seen in chapter 1 the range of difficulties which Paul faced in his apostolic ministry. Now pain comes to him not from external opposition, but from his care for the well-being of fellow believers. Later, in chapter 7, we gain a glimpse of the sleepless nights he endured as he tossed and turned, wondering how his letter had been received and hoping for news from Titus as to how they had responded (7:5–6). And later he will refer to the constant pressure of his concern for all the churches (11:28).

Christian leaders who serve in the spirit of Christ will always feel such pain if they care for others. It is particularly the case when some form of discipline has to be exercised, a wrong has to be confronted or a rebuke has to be administered. Since the church is a human as well as a divine institution, it will always have relational problems that will demand this kind of intervention by wise pastors who will be motivated by love and integrity. But all Christians, whether leaders or not, must aim to express the cluster of qualities which Paul demonstrates: a loving concern for one another which affirms and encourages, but which is also willing to confront appropriately when the occasion demands.

Questions

1. When do you think legitimate discipline by church leaders crosses the boundary to become lording it over others (1:24), and how can this be avoided?

2. Paul implies that God is the witness of our thoughts and actions (1:23). How would being more conscious of this truth impact our lives?

3. Do you think that Christian leaders should show emotion quite the way Paul does?

Paul's Letters to Corinth

There have been many attempts to reconstruct the sequence of visits and letters between Paul and the Corinthians. The pattern of visits is described in the box labelled "Paul's Travel Plans" on page 24. But what of Paul's letters?

Paul probably wrote four letters to the church in Corinth:

Letter 1 was written soon after Paul had left Corinth, following the founding of the church. It addressed some specific issues about Christians relating to fellow believers whose behaviour did not match up to the requirements of the gospel. They were living in a compromised fashion and Paul refers to this in 1 Corinthians 5:9–11. Letter 1 was not preserved, perhaps because it addressed a specific issue for a specific moment and did not really have wider application to the churches.

Letter 2 was written a short while later. Paul had received news of a wide range of concerns within the church and wrote to address these. This is preserved as our 1 Corinthians.

Letter 3 was the "severe" letter we have already referred to earlier in this chapter. The situation in the church had deteriorated, despite Paul's attempts to correct the situation through Letter 2, and so he had decided to make an urgent visit. Letter 3 was then written following this "painful" visit, and it is mentioned in 2 Corinthians 2:4 and 7:8–9.

Letter 4 is our 2 Corinthians, which demonstrates that Paul is deeply concerned about the Corinthians, and longs for a restored relationship with them.

If Letters 2 and 4 are preserved, but Letter 1 was not saved, the question remains: what happened to Letter 3, the "severe letter"? Some people think that perhaps this letter made up chapters 10–13 of 2 Corinthians, a section which shows such a marked change of tone that "severe" would be an appropriate description for it. While this might be possible, there are a number of reasons against this. How 2 Corinthians came to be constructed is dealt with more fully in the box labelled "The Unity of 2 Corinthians" on page 131.

6

Firmness and Forgiveness
2 Corinthians 2:5–11

Discipline in the church must retain a balance between necessary rebuke and pastoral action on the one hand, and forgiveness and acceptance on the other.

The word "discipline" is not common in the vocabulary of today's church. The mood of our age, which stresses tolerance and steers clear of judgment or the allocation of blame, has so influenced us that the thought of disciplining fellow Christians seems strangely out of place today.

The next section will demonstrate how Paul handled a specific case of discipline. It provides further support for the view that, far from being uncaring and dictatorial, Paul is a man of deep compassion. His love is seen not only in the fact that it cost him a great deal to rebuke the Corinthians, but also in his attitude toward a particular offender.

In verse 6, Paul refers to the punishment that had been inflicted on a member of the congregation. Although it is possible that this is a reference to the person whom Paul describes in 1 Corinthians 5 (an immoral brother who had to be expelled from the congregation), it is much more likely that it is a description of someone in the Corinthian church who had offended Paul in some way (see box labelled "The Offender," p. 33). The offender had caused grief for Paul, probably in the form of a public insult, and this not only offended Paul but had wider repercussions.

The Corinthians had disciplined the offender (7:6–13), but Paul was concerned that the matter should be brought to closure with both firmness and forgiveness. His teaching therefore provides us with a helpful model for discipline in our own Christian communities. In these verses there is a sequence of important statements which, properly interpreted and acted upon, will lead to wise pastoral practice for every generation of the church.

1. Failure Has a Corporate Impact (2:5–6)

By virtue of the fact that Christians are one body, the failure of one person affects the entire community. Although it seems as though the offence was directed towards Paul, he indicates that such a failure will have grieved all of them (2:5). An injury inflicted on one person will result in pain being widely felt. There is a domino effect. That is one of the reasons why discipline is necessary.

2. Failure Requires Appropriate Discipline (2:8–9)

The word Paul uses for the discipline that had been exercised is "punishment" (2:6), and this is related to the word "rebuke." It was important that the Corinthians took heed of Paul's "severe letter" and that they had acted as he requested. It was an expression of their obedience to the apostle and therefore of their obedience to God (v. 9). But Paul is now writing to indicate that sufficient discipline has been exercised (v. 6). All discipline needs to be appropriate to the offence, neither too lenient nor too severe.

3. Discipline Should Lead to Generous Forgiveness (2:7–8, 10)

We can all understand why forgiveness is necessary. Perhaps you have had the experience in your family or in the church of being rebuked or confronted with your failure. Whatever the initial problem that calls for discipline, we immediately feel "outside"; we feel condemned by others. We need to know the forgiveness of God, but also the forgiveness of our fellow believers (2:7). But more than that we also need to feel that we belong. We need the positive reaffirmation of their love for us (v. 8).

Paul is careful to demonstrate his own willingness to forgive alongside his call that the Corinthians should forgive the offender (v. 10). To demonstrate the genuineness of his forgiveness, he indicates that he does so in the sight of Christ. He is again seeking to be utterly transparent, recognizing that he lives his life in Christ's presence and therefore must be completely genuine in all his attitudes and actions.

4. Forgiveness Leads to Spiritual Health (2:11)

There is one further reason for demonstrating both discipline and forgiveness, both godly confrontation and the reaffirmation of our love for one another. It is to make sure that Satan does not exploit the situation (2:11). Paul is aware that there was a significant spiritual dimension to the problem. Satan is not passive when it comes to relational breakdown or community fracture. He will often start it off, and he will want to make it worse. We need to be alert to his schemes and be ready, through forgiveness and acceptance, to restore the person who has fallen so that no further spiritual injury is inflicted on the Christian community.

Questions

1. Forgiveness is at the heart of the Christian gospel, but often it is not at the heart of the Christian community. Why do you think that is?

2. Paul says that we are not unaware of Satan's schemes (2:11). What are Satan's most frequent devices in our lives and in our churches?

3. How can we best show love and affirmation towards someone who has failed or offended us, without appearing to condone his or her wrongdoing?

The Offender

Who was the person requiring the discipline to which Paul refers in 2 Corinthians 2? Traditionally, the offender has been linked with the incest case which Paul mentions in 1 Corinthians 5:1, suggesting it was the same man.

But a more likely view is that the offence Paul refers to in 2 Corinthians was some form of open insult or slander against Paul. This probably occurred during Paul's painful visit, and it was one element of the opposition which he encountered.

This view fits more naturally with the tone of Paul's instructions, particularly regarding the punishment that was appropriate to the offence. In 1 Corinthians 5 the guilty party was to be expelled and handed over to Satan, whereas in 2 Corinthians 2:6–8, Paul urges forgiveness and restoration, and deliberately suggests that Satan should not be allowed to make capital out of the situation.

Paul had been concerned that the offence against him could have wider repercussions. It was certainly directed against him, but it affected others too (2 Corinthians 2:5 could read "not only to me" or "not primarily to me"). Through his tearful letter he had urged the Corinthians to take the necessary disciplinary action. At last it seemed that they had obeyed, which is why he now appeals for forgiveness.

Throughout we can detect Paul's generous and compassionate heart, both to the offender and to the church as a whole.

Section 2

Paul Describes His Ministry

2 Corinthians 2:12–7:16

7

Making Christ Known
2 Corinthians 2:12–17

Despite pressures of all kinds, we share the victory of Christ and carry the responsibility of making him known in all circumstances and situations.

The opening verses of this section form a bridge between the explanation of Paul's behaviour, which has so far dominated the first two chapters of Paul's letter, and the next major section which describes Paul's ministry. We are about to embark on a major detour that will last until 7:2. Paul will then pick up where he left off in 2:12 and will return to the issue of the brother who had sinned. But now he begins a section which is a most moving description of true Christian ministry. Before he begins, verses 12 and 13 provide a transition.

We shouldn't miss the simple remark in verse 12 which represents Paul's constant priority: he went to Troas "to preach the gospel of Christ." That was the constant ambition of his life, as we will see in chapter 5. But it is clear that, despite an open door of opportunity, he had no peace of mind, probably because he continued to be concerned about the Corinthians' response to his letter. Clearly Paul was not a cool and dispassionate leader, unaffected by the feelings and responses of others. The response of the Corinthians was very important to him, but he had to wait still longer to discover the results of his pastoral intervention.

He then begins the description of the ministry to which God has called him, and this provides an important introduction to the characteristics of all true Christian service.

1. The Triumph of Christ (2:14)

Despite the pressures Paul had just described, and the inner turmoil of 2:13, he knew there was another side to the story. The image of a triumphal procession (v. 14) could be misleading were we not already familiar with the themes so far in the opening two chapters of Paul's letter. For Paul is not being triumphalistic. He has described the range of pressures which have brought him close to death, the weaknesses which beset his apostolic ministry, and the pain of tough love as he has disciplined the church. It is possible that his description of a triumphal procession is written with a degree of irony. But given his opening phrase, "Thanks be to God" (v. 14), it is more likely that Paul is bursting into praise as he associates himself closely with Christ, in whose fellowship he both suffers and triumphs.

Paul's readers would have been familiar with the Roman processions of victorious armies. Paul is either saying that he is walking in triumph in such a procession, sharing in Christ's victory, or he is implying that he is one of the slaves being led captive by the returning conqueror. Either way, he rejoices in the victory procession of which he is a part. His union with Christ means that despite the overwhelming pressures and hardships which he has described, he gladly serves the Lord Jesus Christ who has won the victory.

2. The Impact of Christian Witness (2:15–16)

Processions also included priests who burnt incense along the route as a form of tribute to the victorious army. Perhaps Paul is picking up this image when he goes on to describe his ministry as spreading the knowledge of Christ much as a fragrance is carried in the wind. Through the demands of his ministry, with all of its crushing burdens, others have detected the fragrance of Christ. In fact, Paul goes on to describe how the knowledge of Christ has two opposite effects. Either it is a fragrance of life to those who are being saved, as they welcome the knowledge of Christ and respond to the gospel; or it is an aroma of death to those who are perishing, who reject the gospel as foolishness and turn away from Christ (2:15–16).

Notice the words he uses: "those who are being saved"; "those who are perishing." The New Testament describes salvation as having a past, present and future dimension, and verse 15 describes a present process. The reaction of people to the fragrance of Christ is confirming either their salvation or their judgment.

It is a serious business. No wonder Paul asks, "And who is equal to such a task?" (v. 16). He will answer that question in the next section (3:5), but it serves to highlight the significance of his witness to Christ and the serious consequences of people's response.

3. The Sincerity of Christian Service (2:17)

Paul again responds to the accusations of the false teachers in Corinth by underlining his own sincerity and transparency. He has handled God's word with absolute integrity, unlike those who "peddle" the word for profit (2:17). He uses a word which means "to corrupt." He is not like a market trader with a bold sales pitch but with shoddy plastic goods. He is not pretending to sell a quality wine while having secretly watered it down the night before. "Unlike so many" implies a deep concern for the welfare of the Corinthian church, in danger of succumbing to the teaching of the pseudo-apostles (see boxes labelled "Paul and the Corinthians," p. 3, and "Paul's Opponents," p. 43), whom Paul saw as deceitful salesmen and fake leaders. Rather, his ministry is characterized by openness ("we speak before God," v. 17) and divine authority ("as those sent from God," v. 17). He will return to similar themes in his defence in chapter 4.

In these three simple statements there are important lessons for all Christians seeking to serve Christ:

- *We live our lives in the light of Christ's victory.* Although we might endure all kinds of hardships for naming the name of Christ, we willingly submit to serve him, and know that in all circumstances ("always," v. 14) we can count on Christ's victory.
- *Our lives communicate the gospel to others*, like an aroma carrying the news of Christ. And if we are doing our job, people will react one way or the other. It seems that neutrality is quite impossible. Either they will be drawn closer to Christ, or their rejection of him will become all the more deliberate. It will result in life for those who believe, and death for those who do not. It is sobering to see our Christian witness in such clear-cut terms, and it encourages us to reflect on our responsibilities with due seriousness.
- *We are accountable to God*, called to serve him by proclaiming his word with honesty and integrity. There should be no shortcuts in our presentation of the gospel, no dilution of the message to make it more palatable, but a sincere presentation of the truth of the gospel through both our lives and our words.

Questions

1. Paul speaks of the "aroma of Christ" in verses 15 and 16. Can people "smell" Christ on us and our church? What "fragrances" combine to form a genuine gospel aroma?

2. Verses 15 and 16 show that rejecting the knowledge of Christ has serious consequences. How can we help non-Christians to understand this?

3. In what ways are Christians tempted to dilute the message to make it more marketable in today's culture (2:17)? How can we strike the balance between a right translation of the message (so that people understand), and a wrong alteration of it (which distorts the truth)?

8

Sufficient Resources

2 Corinthians 3:1–6

> **All believers are equipped and competent for ministry if they are indwelt by the Holy Spirit.**

In the last section Paul had posed a serious question as he described his ministry and calling: "Who is equal to such a task?" (2:16). In this section he responds to that question, as part of a sustained development of a theme which will occupy the whole of chapter 3. Paul is a minister of the new covenant, radically different from the old covenant of the past. Throughout the chapter he will demonstrate the contrasts between these two covenants.

It is likely that part of the background to Paul's concern regarding the intruders in Corinth was their desire to impose Jewish demands on Christian believers. If that was the case, then chapter 3 of Paul's letter responds forcefully to such teaching, as well as providing all subsequent generations with one of the most profound descriptions of the impact of the gospel in transforming our lives.

1. The Evidence of God's Work (3:1–3)

Having described the sincerity of his motives in apostolic ministry, Paul realizes he is opening himself to the charge of boasting (3:1). This will be a recurring theme later in the letter. At this point he is expressing his concern that the Corinthian believers do not seem to support his apostleship, despite all of his work on their behalf. Do they really need further official letters of recommendation? Such letters of introduction were common in Paul's day, and are still used in some Christian circles today, and he is not dismissing their place or value. Rather, he is surprised that such letters of introduction should be needed for the person who had founded the church, the spiritual father of so many of the believers in Corinth! Surely they know that they themselves represent his letter; they are his credentials to be seen as an apostle (v. 2).

There is no need for a formal letter written with ink when there exists an open letter in the form of the Corinthian believers themselves. This letter is written on hearts and it is obvious to everyone (v. 2). They are the real proof of the sincerity and effectiveness of his ministry. And this is the result of the work of the Spirit of the living God (v. 3). It is not a formal letter but a commendation in the form of people made alive by the Spirit.

It is here that Paul begins the contrasts between the old and new covenants. The covenant is the way in which God establishes a relationship with his people. It is grounded in God's character. His purposes for his people, expressed in the law, were written on "tablets of stone" (v. 3). But now, just as the prophets predicted, the Spirit of the living God writes on human hearts. Paul is recalling the promise recorded in Jeremiah 31:33, which anticipated a new covenant when the Lord would put his law in people's minds and write it on their hearts (see box labelled "Covenant," p. 45).

2. The Equipping of God's Spirit (3:4–6)

Should that seem too bold an assertion, Paul underlines that such a ministry is achieved by God himself. He is completely confident about God's work in the lives of the Corinthian believers (3:4), not because of his own skill as a preacher, or any human sufficiency or competence, but because "our competence comes from God" (v. 5).

Paul is not wanting to bolster his own position. He is not engaged in spiritual one-upmanship, boosting his own ego or building his own empire. He is not claiming anything for himself (v. 5). He is underlining that his sufficiency is entirely outside of himself – it is God who has made him competent for such a demanding ministry (vv. 5–6). The capacity to cope with the hardships he has described, the ability to proclaim the gospel in all circumstances, the willingness to bear the awesome responsibility of Christian witness and even the fruits of his labours there in Corinth – all this was the result of God's Spirit.

Such verses are important for Christians serving the Lord today. Paul's reminder of the sufficiency of God's resources is an encouragement to those who feel their inadequacy in Christian ministry, but also a timely reminder to those who take pride in their service. We are completely dependent on God; whenever there is fruit from our work, the praise belongs to him.

Paul is even more explicit: "He has made us competent as ministers of a new covenant" (v. 6). In the past, God had given the law to the people through Moses, written on tablets of stone. But because of their inability to keep that law it was effectively a letter that killed. It condemned rather than liberated. Now, Paul's ministry of the new covenant was to bring the gospel, which by God's Holy Spirit produced a life-giving and life-changing result in all who believed. His ministry was not of the letter but of the Spirit. In the next section Paul embarks on a profound explanation of that new covenant ministry, a ministry which we share as those proclaiming that same gospel and empowered by that same life-giving Spirit.

Questions

1. To what extent is your life a legible and accurate letter from Christ to be read by people around you? What is its message? How is that message seen and heard?

2. Is it still possible in today's church for the "letter to kill" (3:6)? What do you think this might mean today, and how can this be avoided?

3. Discuss and note down how Paul's example encourages you forward in Christian service.

Paul's Opponents

Have you ever tried to make sense of a conversation by listening to someone speaking to a friend on the phone? The problem is that you hear only one side of the story. You have to piece together the conversation on the basis of the responses of the person you can hear. Discovering what the problems were in Corinth is rather like that. We have only Paul's remarks, but nevertheless the picture begins to become clear as we study his defence and his sharp rebukes.

The letter is all about relationships. Paul loved the believers in Corinth. He had founded the church, and any sign of immaturity or disorder or sin within that community caused him considerable pain.

It is clear that his relationship with the church was very shaky and vulnerable. What makes it such a moving letter is the very personal way in which Paul opens his heart and life to their scrutiny, describing at times his own confusion and emotional turmoil, but also his longing that they should be reconciled.

Why was all this needed? Piecing together the jigsaw, it seems clear that new teachers had arrived in Corinth who were opposing Paul and were winning the support of many of the believers. Who were they? We know that they were Jewish (2 Cor 11:12) and that they were from out of town (11:4). They were intruding in Paul's sphere of ministry (10:12–18), and they were even supported financially by the church.

Paul's response demonstrates that there were two main issues. One was that Paul faced a character assassination. The new teachers were clearly making a devastating assault on his suitability to be an apostle, and Paul replies to this in various sections of the letter. The criticism of his leadership is seen in Paul's responses in such sections as 1:12–14, 17, 23–24; 2:17; 3:1; 4:2; 5:11–13; 6:3; 7:2; 8:20. The second issue related to the seriously flawed teaching which the newcomers had introduced. It is very likely that the new teachers wanted to impose on the Christians in Corinth some Jewish regulations from the law of Moses. They are referred to as "Judaizers" in many commentaries. (See also Gal 2:11–16.)

The first attack concerned apostolic leadership. The newcomers were keen on special "spiritual" experiences and supernatural power and, in common with the travelling magicians of the time, charged fees for their services. Some were influenced by Greek culture and were impressed by eloquence. In other words, their view of leadership was shaped by the standards of the secular gurus of the day. When they looked at Paul, he seemed little more than a clown. He was a manual worker, and an amateur speaker who didn't even charge for his services – what kind of leader was that? Paul's response not only represents a devastating assault on the pretentious claims of such false teachers but has provided us with an abiding model of true Christian service from which every generation of the church can learn.

The second attack is no less serious, not least because it represented a "different Jesus" and a "different gospel" (see also Gal 1:6–7). To try to impose Jewish regulations on the grace of the gospel was to attack its heart, and Paul's careful explanation of the superiority of the covenant and the centrality of Christ's reconciling death gives us one of the greatest explanations of the glory of the gospel of Jesus Christ.

Covenant

"Covenant" is an important word used throughout the Bible to describe an agreement made by God with his people for the purpose of securing a lasting relationship with them. It first appears in connection with Abraham, and God's promise to him to "be your God," and also to his offspring after him (Gen 17:1–7). This covenant was further expressed through the giving of the law (Exod 32:15), which, as Paul demonstrates in 2 Corinthians 3, failed through the inability of people to keep it. In that sense, Paul says, it brought death and condemnation. The Old Testament nevertheless spoke of a new covenant, which was anticipated by the prophets and was granted by God to his disobedient people. Jeremiah prophesied that the new covenant would be written on the hearts and minds of the people (Jer 31:31–40; see also Isa 55:3; Jer 32:40; 50:5; Ezek 34:25).

Several of the prophets also link the promised new covenant with the ministry of the Spirit, as Paul does in 2 Corinthians 3. Speaking through Ezekiel, the Lord promises: "I will give you a new heart and put a new spirit in you; I will remove from you your heart of stone and give you a heart of flesh. And I will put my Spirit in you and move you to follow my decrees and be careful to keep my laws" (Ezek 36:24–38; see also Isa 59:21).

The New Testament acknowledges that the Gentiles, originally excluded from the covenant (Eph 2:12), are now brought into God's family through the work of Christ. This is why Paul describes the new covenant as "more glorious" in 2 Corinthians 3, because now it is founded on Christ's redeeming work and empowered by his Spirit. It results in life and holiness.

9

Greater Glory
2 Corinthians 3:7–11

> The ministry of the gospel is far more glorious than the old covenant and has life-transforming consequence.

Just as the last section sought to answer the question of 2:16, "Who is equal to such a task?," so this section answers the question of 3:8, "Will not the ministry of the Spirit be even more glorious?" Paul continues to highlight the contrast between the old and new covenant, and does so through the use of the idea of "glory."

So far Paul has demonstrated that the glory of his ministry does not coincide with the expectations of the false apostles in Corinth. Far from it! He has rehearsed his difficulties, not his successes; he has spoken of his experiences of shame and dishonour, not of great personal achievements and human glory. To help the Corinthians understand how his ministry really is glorious, he compares old and new covenants using a form of argument that was common in his day. If the old was glorious, how much more glorious is the new!

Paul has in mind the account of Moses in the book of Exodus. The old covenant was expressed through the written law "engraved in letters on stone" (v. 7). Moses would speak with the Lord, and after that encounter his face would shine with reflected glory (Exod 34:29–31). Paul explains that the Israelites couldn't look at Moses's face, even though that glory was "fading" or "set aside" in comparison with the glory of Jesus. The old covenant, then, as expressed in the law given to Moses, was a revelation of God's glory because it expressed God's character. But now, with the coming of the Spirit of God, there is a far greater revelation of God's glory. And it is this ministry of the Spirit which Paul shows us, in all his weakness and suffering.

As Paul reflects on the old and new covenants, he draws three clear contrasts in this section.

1. Life, Not Death (3:7–8)

The first contrast is one he has touched on in the previous section. The law is like a pane of glass. One failure means that the whole pane is shattered. In Moses's day the people rebelled against the law God had given, and even though it was designed to be life-giving, their failure meant it became an instrument of death.

So, Paul argues, if even that revelation through the old covenant was glorious, how much more glorious is the ministry of the Spirit which brings life!

2. Righteousness, Not Condemnation (3:9–10)

Second, the failure of God's people to keep his law brought with it condemnation. If that covenant can still be described as glorious, how much more glorious is the ministry of the gospel which produces not condemnation but righteousness (3:9)! Here Paul is introducing a theme which he will expound more fully in chapter 5. The gospel of which he is a minister is a glorious revelation of the righteous God who forgives, the God who does not count people's sins against them (5:19). This is the heart of the good news which Paul proclaimed. Whereas the law ministers death and condemnation, the gospel ministers life and righteousness.

3. Permanent, Not Transient (3:10–11)

Third, the old covenant pales by comparison with the new. The gospel is so glorious that, in effect, the law now has no glory (3:10). It is impossible to see the light of the candle when it is placed in the full glare of the sun's rays. The glory of the law effectively vanishes when compared with Jesus, the light of the world. This, Paul says, is a glory which lasts (v. 11). What Christ has achieved in the gospel will last for eternity. And in our lives the Holy Spirit has applied Christ's work, bringing life and righteousness. He is the deposit (5:5), guaranteeing that the work will finally be completed. His presence in our lives is the characteristic feature of the new covenant ministry which Paul is describing.

If any of Paul's readers were tempted to go back to Jewish rules and regulations, they must have been pulled up short by his teaching in this section. Paul is demonstrating that his gospel ministry, the ministry of the Spirit, could not be more glorious. It might not be the glory which the false teachers had in mind, but with all of his weakness, look what his ministry is achieving! Life, not death; righteousness, not condemnation; permanent glory, not a fading glory – because it is a glory within every believer. And now, through the gospel, we are not excluded from God's presence and his glory is no longer veiled. We no longer need to bring sacrifices, for in Christ a new covenant has been secured, a new and living way has been opened up.

Sometimes Christians today fail to live in the light of that glorious new covenant ministry. They imagine that they must work hard to impress God, or they seek special experiences in the hope of winning his approval. But they fail to see that all that is necessary for our justification has been achieved by Christ on the cross. And therein lies the paradox which is at the heart of the gospel and at the heart of Paul's letter to the Corinthians: the cross is the best place to see God's glory! Paul's ministry and ours will be glorious, not because of our success or achievement, but when we direct people to Christ and his cross and live our lives by that same pattern of death and resurrection in union with him (for further comments, see box labelled "Glory," p. 54).

Questions

1. In what ways might you still be tempted to live as if you had to earn God's approval?

2. "We have seen his glory," the disciples said about Jesus (John 1:14). How did Jesus show "glory" in his life? Can we show the same glory?

3. Moses's face shone because God spoke to him "face to face, as one speaks to a friend" (Exod 33:11). In what sense can we be friends of God, or is that reserved for special people like Moses and Paul? Make a list of the ways in which our friendship with God might be expressed.

10

An Open and Shut Case
2 Corinthians 3:12–18

Christians have been liberated and transformed by the Holy Spirit and now demonstrate an ever-increasing glory that leads to Christlikeness.

Having established that the ministry of the Spirit has such powerful and permanent effects, Paul says that he can be completely confident in his preaching of the gospel of hope. Boldness (3:12) was a characteristic of Paul and the early Christians, as it will be for all Christians who have grasped the certainties of the gospel ministry to which Paul has referred.

1. Open Ministry (3:12–13)

Because of his boldness, Paul is completely open in his ministry (the word for "bold" implies "speaking openly" and could even mean "bare-faced"). He has nothing to hide. Here he picks up once again the story of Moses, and this section is a commentary on Exodus 34:29–35. Moses placed a veil over his face. Exodus suggests that the people could not look on such glory, and Paul adds in 2 Corinthians 3:13 that the veil was to hide the fact that the radiance was fading away. Even such fading glory was something which sinful people could not look at.

It is possible that Paul implies here that because of the veil over Moses's face, the people could not see the glory finally fade, or understand what the end purpose of such fading glory really was. The old covenant was temporary, pointing to something greater. But they couldn't see it. By contrast, Paul and the apostles could be quite "barefaced" in their proclamation of the gospel. They could use great boldness of speech (v. 12), for they knew that the new covenant ministry was permanent and life-giving.

2. Closed Minds (3:14–15)

In Moses's day, the people could not grasp the significance of the fading glory. Paul describes this in 3:14: "Their minds were made dull." There was a spiritual insensitivity, and Paul indicates that this remains the case for many Jews. Whenever the Old Testament is read, the same veil is drawn across their minds, and they are unable to see the truth to which the old covenant is pointing. This represented a painful reality for Paul, who identified closely with his own people, the Jews, and felt a desperate sadness that they rejected the Christ whom he had met on the Damascus road.

We know that Paul is describing not just Jewish unbelief, but also the mind-set of all men and women who are rejecting the truth as it is in Jesus. No-one can understand the gospel simply through intellectual reasoning. As Paul writes in chapter 4, people's minds are blinded, so that they cannot see the truth (4:4). In 3:14 Paul refers to dull minds and in 3:15 he refers to veiled hearts. Sinful rebellion and unbelief have deep-set consequences, affecting everything about us. It takes a supernatural intervention to change this.

3. The Lord's Work of Illumination (3:16)

It is not until a person turns to the Lord that the veil is taken away. When a Jew comes to see that the old covenant is superseded by the new – that grace and truth came by Jesus Christ (John 1:17) – then the veil is removed. And so it is for all, Jew and Gentile alike, who turn to Christ.

4. The Spirit's Work of Liberation (3:17)

Here is a nugget of Paul's teaching, a guiding principle in his theology: "Where the Spirit of the Lord is, there is freedom." When people turn to the Lord (3:16), they are set free from the bondage to the law. More than that, as Paul expounds in his letter to the Romans, they are set free from sin and death. Written codes of conduct, the letter of the law, are powerless to change our lives and liberate us from the bondage of our sinfulness and disobedience. It is the work of the

Spirit of God to show us our need, apply Christ's work in our lives, and set us free to serve him.

5. The Spirit's Work of Transformation (3:18)

This section culminates in a profound expression of Christian privilege. Verse 18 should be read alongside verse 13, where Paul describes the veiled face of Moses. That glory was fading, as we have seen, but now we are being transformed into Christ's likeness "with ever-increasing glory." That glory is no longer for the one person, Moses, but is for all Christians. It is not a glory to be covered, but one which we all reflect with unveiled faces. The verse could read either "reflect" or "behold" the Lord's glory, and both seem appropriate. For now we see the glory of the Lord, into whose presence Christ has brought us. And in turn, we reflect that glory in the world and to one another, as those called to be like Christ.

Paul has described Jews reading the Old Testament with veiled hearts. But true believers, with unveiled faces, can see in the mirror of the gospel the true glory of Christ. The transformation which Paul describes sums up God's purpose for our lives. We are to be changed day by day into Christ's likeness. That life-long process comes about only as we focus our attention on Christ, and the Spirit works within us (v. 18b). It is the Spirit who opens our hearts and minds, who liberates us through the gospel and who now transforms us day by day into Christ's likeness with ever-increasing glory.

This is the climax of Paul's argument about the superiority of the new covenant, and it provides us with a profound description not just of Paul's ministry but of our own. We who have been transformed in this way must now be ministers of that gospel, reflecting the glory of the crucified and risen Lord into whose image we are being changed. Our ministry will have the same characteristics of dying and rising, and it is to this challenge that Paul now turns in chapter 4.

Questions

1. What do you think is the connection between hope and boldness (3:12)?

2. "Where the Spirit of the Lord is, there is freedom" (3:17). How do you think this is seen in our personal lives and in the local church?

3. Paul talks about a profound transformation taking place in our lives. In what ways have you seen such change in your life or in the lives of fellow Christians in your church? (It's worth remembering that others may be more aware of changes in you than you are yourself!)

Glory

The word the biblical writers use to describe the majesty and dazzling brightness of God is "glory." We human beings cannot see him face to face, but he allows us to see him in his glory. It is objective and visible. For example, God's glory is seen in all that he has made (Ps 19:1), in Jesus's miracles (John 2:11) and, most significantly, in Jesus's death (John 12:23–24; 17:4).

It is as we see the revelation of God's glory that we worship him. We "glorify" him through our grateful thanksgiving and committed obedience (Rom 4:20; 15:5–6, 9; 1 Cor 6:20; 10:31). The usual New Testament Greek word for glory is *doxa*, and a word we use for giving God glory in worship is *doxology*.

But God's glory is not only something which we are to seek, and which provokes our response of worship. God also imparts his glory to his people. In 2 Corinthians 4:6, we see how Paul describes the way in which, through the gospel, God shines his light into our dark hearts. And in chapter 3 we see how the Holy Spirit is actively at work revealing God's glory in our lives with ever greater intensity (2 Cor 3:17–18). In other words, we begin to reflect the likeness of Jesus himself. We are revealing God's glory.

How incredible that the awesome and holy God, whose unapproachable majesty marks him out as the King of glory, is also the one who by his Spirit is graciously at work to transform us into his likeness! We are part of the eternal glory of the new creation about which we will read more at the end of 2 Corinthians 4.

11

Realistic Ministry
2 Corinthians 4:1–6

Being a minister of the gospel is a great privilege. Paul describes the qualities of faithful ministry and the challenges and changes we can expect to accompany such ministry.

Having drawn out some of the key differences between the old and new covenants, Paul now writes about the minister of that new covenant. A minister is simply someone called to serve; although some churches use the term to describe their full-time pastor, it is a word which belongs to all who are faithful in their determination to share the gospel. Paul's ministry, and that of all Christians, will be marked by distinct features which he introduces in this section.

1. Dependence: Trusting God's Mercy (4:1)

If we had to identify the greatest challenge facing Christians today, it might not necessarily be militant Islam, or an aggressive atheism, or occult activity. It is most likely to be plain and simple discouragement. Most of us pass through times when we are under pressure to give in, tempted to feel that our work is no longer worthwhile.

Twice in this chapter Paul explains that he doesn't give in to such discouragement. "We do not lose heart" (4:1, 16). It was by God's mercy (v. 1) that Paul had been entrusted with his ministry and, as we have seen from 1:1, his sense of stewardship and responsibility moved him to get on with the job with determination and courage. Our Christian ministry does not depend on our own strength, but on God's faithfulness towards us. Christians have both a sense of compulsion but also a sense of encouragement arising from their high calling to be stewards of the glorious ministry of reconciliation. Paul has explained in chapter 3 what that new covenant ministry is all about. Now we should be motivated by our God-given responsibility to serve him and encouraged by the fact he will provide all we need for the task.

2. Faithfulness: Setting Forth the Truth (4:2)

Christian ministry is also characterized by its directness. Paul had already written that he acted towards the Corinthians with integrity (1:12–17). Now he underlines that this is a basic feature of all his ministry. Unlike his critics, he was completely transparent; everything was above board (4:2). He was not one person in private and another in public. He used no cunning or craftiness, and he refused to distort the message. As he has already stated in 2:17, he did not dilute the word of God, or make it conform to any party interest. Instead, he gave his energies to "setting forth the truth plainly" (4:2).

Perhaps you have seen a conjuror, showing his hand to the audience. He wants to show that he is holding nothing back, concealing nothing up his sleeves. Unlike the conjuror, Paul reveals his hand with transparent openness; he has no intention whatsoever of deceiving his audience. His task is to proclaim faithfully the whole counsel of God.

Only this open proclamation of the truth reaches a person's conscience (v. 2). We should never give up, imagining that God's word can't reach a person's heart. And neither should we fall into the mistake of thinking that anything other than the truth will reach them. Like Paul, we should be committed to the courageous proclamation of the gospel, whatever the audience and however tempting it might be to modify the message for our comfort, or security, or even for our personal advance. Paul's ministry is to be faithful to that message, a servant for Jesus's sake (v. 5).

3. Realism: Understanding Spiritual Realities (4:3–4)

Paul is under no illusions as to what this faithfulness will mean. Many people who hear the gospel will write it off as totally irrelevant. Jesus's parable of the sower warns us that the word will be "received" in different ways. For some people the gospel is effectively hidden. It is veiled, Paul says, "to those who are perishing" (4:3). Paul is quite realistic: he does not underestimate the enemy, the "god of this age" who "has blinded the minds of unbelievers" (v. 4).

There is always a danger that Christian ministry can adopt a certain professionalism, so that it becomes a matter of routine. We have our styles of ministry, well-rehearsed and delivered, our evangelistic programmes and contemporary presentations at our fingertips. But we can make the serious mistake of underestimating the spiritual battle. We forget that we are not conveying the truth in a sympathetic or even neutral environment. There are hostile forces actively at work, preventing people from seeing the truth.

This is a characteristic of the age in which we live (v. 4), and it presents us with a sober challenge. For one thing, we shouldn't be indifferent about it, since those whose minds are blinded "are perishing" (v. 3). Only the light of the gospel can save them. For another, we should devote ourselves to presenting Christ with an urgency and prayerfulness that will, by God's grace, break through this blindness.

4. Priority: Proclaiming Jesus Christ as Lord (4:5–6)

With his usual directness Paul stresses the heart of this Godgiven ministry: "For what we preach is not ourselves, but Jesus Christ as Lord" (4:5). Paul was not wanting to parade his own interests or opinions or to start a personality cult. He was faithful to his calling by being faithful to the message, to which Christ was central (vv. 4–5). There is no other possible stance for the person called to proclaim Christ. Not only am I to ensure that Christ, and not myself, is at the centre, I am also to be a servant of others in that task: "and ourselves as your servants for Jesus' sake" (v. 5). Christian ministers should be more at home with a washbasin and towel than standing centre stage.

As we do our part in proclaiming Christ, Paul expresses the assurance of God's illuminating work. He draws his illustration from God's work in creation (v. 6). God spoke, and order came out of chaos; light dispelled the darkness. In the same way, he speaks his word of truth in our hearts, dispelling darkness through "the light of the knowledge of God's glory displayed in the face of Christ" (v. 6). It is possible that Paul is also thinking of his experience on the Damascus road (Acts 9:1–9). The illuminating power of the gospel that day had completely transformed him.

This section shows that Christ is at the centre of all true Christian ministry. It is "the gospel that displays the glory of Christ, who is the image of God" (2 Cor 4:4); it is a preaching of Jesus Christ as Lord (v. 5); it is an experience of the glory of God "in the face of Christ" (v. 6); and our ministry in proclaiming

that glorious gospel is the essence of our service to others "for Jesus' sake" (v. 5).
It is always a temptation to the church to lose the centrality of Christ. All too
easily we focus on programmes, personalities or a range of secondary issues,
when our primary calling is to make Christ known. He must always be at the
centre. That is the heart of Christian ministry.

Questions

1. What are the kinds of things that discourage us in Christian
   service, and how do these verses help us in such circumstances?

2. In what ways might we be tempted to "distort the word of God"
   (4:2), or to preach ourselves (v. 5) rather than Christ?

3. C. S. Lewis once said we can make one of two equal and
   opposite errors when it comes to thinking about Satan: we think
   of him either too much or too little. What is the right balance
   in practice?

4. The most obvious feature of this passage is its clear focus on Jesus
   Christ. Why was Paul so insistent that this Christ-centredness
   should be at the heart of Christian service?

12

Life in Christ
2 Corinthians 4:7–15

> Being "in Christ" is the main principle of Christian living. It helps us come to terms with weakness, it strengthens our faith and it fills us with hope.

As Paul writes about the glory of the gospel, he is inevitably reminded by contrast of his own frailty and weakness. Indeed, this section is the key to much of the letter. Paul's identity was rooted in his experience of Christ.

1. Weakness and Power (4:7–9)

Paul uses an illustration in 4:7 to heighten the contrast between the glory and power of the message and the weakness of the messenger. A cheap pottery lamp will carry the light, and the more the lamp is cracked, the more the light will be seen. Or perhaps Paul has in mind an ordinary clay pot in which would be placed the valuable treasure gained after victory. His purpose is to emphasize the contrast which runs right through the letter: on the one hand, the majesty and power of the gospel message, and on the other, the weak, buffeted and fragile messenger.

The reason for this contrast is expressed in verse 7. It is "to show that this all-surpassing power is from God and not from us." Paul was a good example of this principle. As far as we can tell, in terms of physical appearance he was hardly Superman. His speech might not have been up to much, and in his first letter to the Corinthians he described his nervousness as he came to them: "I came to you in weakness with great fear and trembling. My message and my preaching were not with wise and persuasive words, but with a demonstration of the Spirit's power, so that your faith might not rest on human wisdom, but on God's power" (1 Cor 2:3–5). In his present letter he has already described his sense of desperation in Asia, and the way in which God took him to this extreme point so that "we might not rely on ourselves but on God" (2 Cor 1:9).

In fact, Paul was glad of his weaknesses (12:9), because if people were converted to Christ it was clearly the result of the power of God (1 Cor 2:5). This strange way of working – God's power expressed in the weakness of the messenger – is the heart of the gospel itself (1 Cor 1:20–25). To reinforce the point, Paul draws a series of comparisons in verses 8 and 9. The experiences he is hinting at are spelled out in more detail in the catalogue of suffering recorded later in the letter (2 Cor 11:23–33). Here he summarizes with four pairs of contrasts.

I remember once seeing a message on the side of an ice cream van. It read: "Luigi's ice cream – often licked, but never beaten." This is the kind of play on words which Paul uses in the four comparisons he draws in verses 8 and 9:

- *Hard pressed, but not crushed.* This could be compared to boxing, where the fighter is given very little room to manoeuvre but is not driven into a corner or knocked out. In order to capture Paul's play on words some have suggested a paraphrase such as "hemmed in but not hamstrung."
- *Perplexed, but not in despair.* As Paul wrote in chapter 1, even though he was despairing of life itself, he knew God could be relied upon. The bewilderment of his suffering did not mean complete capitulation. As James Denney paraphrases the play on words, he was "put to it but not utterly put out."[1]
- *Persecuted, but not abandoned.* The suggestion behind Paul's use of "persecuted" is of a person being hunted down or pursued. He knew what it was to be hunted by humans but he was never abandoned by God.
- *Struck down, but not destroyed.* The colloquial rendering might be "knocked down, but not knocked out," or "often felled but never finished."

---

1. Quoted in R. V. G. Tasker, *2 Corinthians*, Tyndale New Testament Commentary (London: Tyndale Press, 1958), 73.

In other words, the end of our human resources does not represent the end of God's (as we also saw in chapter 1). Paul had discovered that his weakness was not only matched (and more than matched) by God's power, but that weakness was the best way to discover such power. Indeed, all Christian ministry must face up to this paradox: weakness is an essential precondition for God's power to be displayed. These moments of pressure, far from being unwelcome intrusions in our lives, should be welcomed as the best opportunities for proving God's power.

The Dutch Christian, Betsie ten Boom, testified to God's sustaining power in the midst of the horrors of Ravensbruck concentration camp, during the Second World War, and expressed the sentiment which Paul is describing in these verses: "There is no pit so deep that God is not deeper still."[2]

2. Union with Christ (4:10–12)

The next verses (4:10–12) sum up the argument of verses 7–9. Paul has already explained that suffering in the Christian life is a direct consequence of being linked to Christ: his sufferings overflow into our lives (1:5). Here in chapter 4, he makes the same point about our identity as believers. Our experience of pressure is nothing other than a reflection of the dying life of Jesus (v. 10). It is not an occasional occurrence, but a constant characteristic of what it means to be united to Christ ("always" occurs in verses 10 and 11).

In the same way, just as Jesus's death was followed by resurrection as a demonstration of the power of God, so Paul's union with Christ meant that he would experience that same renewing power. He was sharing his Master's earthly experience. Four times in verses 10 and 11 he refers to "Jesus," specially emphasizing his humanity. And it would not only be Paul who experienced that renewing power. His experience of the death of Jesus would result in life for the Corinthians (v. 12). That's a real test of the genuineness of our concern for others! He seems to imply that the more he suffers, the more they will experience of Christ's risen life: "All this is for your benefit" (v. 15).

We are back to the main theme of the letter, and it is this: since our life is bound up with Christ's, there is no avoiding such weakness. We should suspect all models of the Christian life or of Christian service which try to avoid weakness or minimize its place in our daily experience. Paul's service was costly because it was "for Jesus' sake" (v. 11). But these demanding experiences

---

2. Recorded by her sister, Corrie Ten Boom, with John and Elizabeth Sherrill, *The Hiding Place* (London: Hodder & Stoughton, 1972).

of weakness were the very occasions for experiencing the living God. Paul says much the same in 13:4: "For to be sure, he was crucified in weakness, yet he lives by God's power. Likewise, we are weak in him, yet by God's power we will live with him to serve you."

3. Why It's All Worthwhile (4:13–15)

This central idea of the value of weakness governs Paul's attitude about the pressures he has just described, and it certainty leads him to state three important and moving conclusions.

First, on the basis of that trust in Jesus, Paul could continue his ministry of proclaiming the gospel. Even if it was a costly experience in terms of personal suffering, he could not remain silent. In 4:13 he quotes Psalm 116:10, where the psalmist had been delivered from a near-death experience and its consequent devastating emotional impact – very similar, perhaps, to the experience Paul has already described in chapter 1. God had delivered the psalmist, and God had delivered Paul. So, he was determined not to give up, but to continue his ministry with that same spirit of faith as the psalmist. It should be our motto too: "I believed, therefore I have spoken" (v. 13).

The next positive conclusion is stated in verse 14, with the same sense of confidence. He would stick to his work of proclaiming the gospel, through all the ups and downs, because he knew it was deeply worthwhile. He knew where it would all end. He was absolutely convinced that one day he would be in God's presence, along with the Corinthian believers, because God would raise them up with Jesus (v. 14). The pressures would be gone, the suffering over. His ministry would be complete and there in heaven would be the fruit of his labours, the Corinthian believers and all who had trusted Christ through his ministry. Interestingly, once again he stresses it is all to do with our identity in Christ: we will be raised up "with Jesus."

His third conclusion is that all the trials which he presently endures are for the benefit of the Corinthians and for the glory of God. Here is another glimpse of the size of Paul's heart and the purity of his motives. Being a minister of the gospel was a tough job; it cost Paul all he had. Yet he could face these hardships because he was not in the business for personal gain, but for the benefit of others. It was for their sake (vv. 5, 15) because it was for Jesus's sake (v. 11). Not only that, it resulted ultimately in the only thing that really mattered: God's glory (v. 15).

The sequence in verse 15 is a lovely description of the impact of the gospel. It is God's grace at work once again. That grace reaches more and more people, the result of which is more and more thanksgiving. And such thanksgiving overflows into a greater declaration of the glory of God. It was this sequence that made it all worthwhile for Paul, and it can make all the difference for us too. We can put up with a great deal if we know that the end result will be God's grace impacting more lives, God's people rejoicing in his victories and God's glory being the eventual goal of all we have passed through.

Questions

1. We tend to think that our weaknesses will mean we will not be able to serve Christ as we should or that they might hinder the advance of the gospel. In what ways do these verses change that perspective?

2. Despite all kinds of pressures, in these verses Paul expresses his certainties. Make a list of these certainties and see if you can turn them into a statement of belief for today, beginning "We believe . . ."

3. What does 4:15 suggest about reasons for worship? (See also 1:10–11.) How can we ensure that worship arises out of a living experience of God's grace?

13

The Real World

2 Corinthians 4:16–18

> The world around us is not what it seems. Paul uses
> three contrasts to show us what really matters.

Christians are sometimes accused of being too heavenly minded to be of any earthly use. This rarely applies to the true Christian, and certainly would not be an apt description of Paul. He was constantly inspired by what lay ahead, and he found great strength for his day-by-day ministry from having an eternal perspective. It is never easy for Christians today to hold this view. We are frequently pushed into thinking that our real life is here and now, and this affects our values, ambitions and attitudes.

Using three sets of contrasts, Paul turns our attention to true reality: the reality of eternity. It is this perspective which once again provokes the expression "we do not lose heart" (4:16). Paul used the identical phrase in verse 1 of this chapter, where it was the glorious ministry of the new covenant which encouraged him forward. Here in verse 16 the motivation for his ministry is the thought of what God is doing in him – and in all true believers – as he looks at eternal realities.

Paul describes three significant contrasts in verses 16–18.

1. Outward Decline and Inward Renewal (4:16)

We need hardly be reminded that our bodies are decaying, that "outwardly we are wasting away" (4:16). Despite our best efforts, the trend is irreversible.

Whether we try jogging, aerobics, slimming or hair-colouring, we cannot halt the decline. One day we will return to dust. As Paul thinks about the experiences he has been describing earlier in the chapter – which resulted in carrying in his body the death of Jesus – his present physical life feels vulnerable and frail. It leads him to emphasize the renewing power of God to which he has already referred. In contrast to the deterioration he felt outwardly, the real Paul was being renewed day by day.

Our inner life, which chapter 4 describes as a life in Christ, can keep fresh, increasing in power and vitality. It is clear that Paul is continuing the theme of weakness and power which he has addressed earlier in the chapter. Our frailty as we grow older can be the occasion for an inner renewal by God's power. This contrast is frequently seen in older people. Non-Christians can sometimes become sour and bitter as they grow older, thinking only of small matters and selfish concerns as their horizons shrink. When I was a student, I visited an eighty-year-old Christian each week. Living on his own, he expressed his gratitude to me for my friendship. But it was I who benefited most from the relationship, for hearing him describe his Christian faith, his hopes for heaven and his prayers for God's work worldwide was deeply encouraging. His outward decline was obvious, but his inward renewal was a most impressive feature of the real person.

2. Present Trouble and Future Glory (4:17)

With what we might regard as surprising understatement, Paul describes his sufferings as "light and momentary" (4:17). We have already seen that his sufferings were real, painful and extensive. But Christian suffering, however painful, is only for this present life and, compared to everlasting glory, it is insignificant.

Paul does more than contrast present suffering and future glory. He indicates that suffering "achieves" something for the future. This needs to be linked with verse 18, where our sufferings encourage us to have the eternal perspective, fixing our eyes, our ambitions, our efforts, on the things that will last forever.

Paul frequently makes the link between suffering and glory. It is part of the theme he has already addressed: we experience both suffering and glory because of our unity with Christ. Paul's testimony in this chapter is that troubles are an inevitable consequence of our fellowship with Christ. So too, we are guaranteed a home in heaven, an eternal glory that "far outweighs" our troubles.

Paul has earlier described his pressures weighing down upon him. But from the perspective of eternity, such troubles are light. Soon Paul will experience the weight of God's glory. His troubles are momentary; his experience of glory will be eternal. And this leads to his third contrast.

3. The Seen and the Unseen (4:18)

Our world places great emphasis on treasure on earth rather than treasure in heaven. For many people around us, especially in Western societies, the prevailing philosophy is "Eat, drink and be merry, for tomorrow we diet!" They are concerned only to maximize their present experience. For many people, all religions are mocked by the hard, white smile of the skull. So now is the time to accumulate, now is the time to enjoy. For Christians to think differently, a radical change of perspective is called for. This is possible only as we fix our eyes not on what is seen but on what is unseen.

Jesus explained in the Beatitudes (Matt 5:3–10) that his values were not of this world; they were kingdom values. He had crept into life's shop window and swopped the price tags round, so that those things which were of great value were now of little value, and those things of little value were now of great value. Learning to value the unseen, the eternal, is part of our Christian discipleship, and Paul explains that our troubles will help us to do this. They help us to see that this world, and our physical bodies, are decaying as a result of sin, and that what really matters is inner renewal and eternal glory.

Questions

1. What does the process of inner renewal mean to you? How can it be deepened in our lives?

2. What does heaven mean to you? Write down your thoughts about it and compare your notes with others. Does it make any serious difference to how you live?

3. How can we overcome the strong pressure of our culture, which stresses the importance of "the seen," the material world? What does Paul mean when he says we should fix our eyes on the unseen? Think of some practical examples.

14

Our Future Home
2 Corinthians 5:1–5

> **Christians need not fear death, for God has prepared a new home for us and has given us the Spirit as a guarantee.**

Michio Kaku is a professor of theoretical physics, and he wrote the following in a chapter entitled "To Live Forever?" in his book *Visions*:

> Anyone who has ever stared in a mirror and watched the inexorable spread of wrinkles, sagging features, and greying hair has yearned for perpetual youth at some point.... No matter how rich, powerful, glamorous or influential you might be, to confront ageing is to confront the reality of your mortality.[1]

While they might be able to improve life's quality and its length, scientists see no answer to the problem of death. We continue to live in its shadow.

In the closing verses of the previous chapter, Paul has written about the importance of viewing life from a different perspective. In contrast to the decay and suffering of this present temporary existence, he has spoken of inner renewal, future glory and an eternal perspective (4:16–18). Perhaps for the first time Paul has begun to confront his own mortality (see also 1:8). We have already seen that he had frequently been close to death in his missionary work, and, having experienced the pressures which this letter catalogues, perhaps

---

1. Michio Kaku, *Visions: How Science Will Revolutionize the 21st Century and Beyond* (Oxford: Oxford University Press, 1998), 201.

69

he was beginning to conclude that he would die before Christ returned. But such a prospect does not fill him with dread or paralyse his present ministry. It was quite the reverse, as this next section shows.

He continues to reflect on the Christian's future hope, explaining that in the face of death we can live with confidence, and through the experience of suffering we can anticipate future glory. These verses are full of positive assurance.

1. We Will Have New Bodies (5:1–3)

As a tentmaker, one illustration immediately came to Paul's mind. Having been through a great deal of physical suffering, he realized his body was fragile and vulnerable. One day, it would be folded up like a tent. But he was absolutely certain ("we know" in 5:1 is written with emphasis) that such a frail tent would be replaced by something much more secure and lasting, designed and built by God himself. It would be "an eternal house in heaven."

Paul has already spoken in 1 Corinthians 15 of the centrality of Jesus's resurrection to the Christian life and Christian hope. Because of our union with Christ, we too will have resurrection bodies. This will be God's work, as Paul stresses in the opening verse of this chapter: "not built by human hands" (5:1). He said the same in the previous chapter: "We know that the one who raised the Lord Jesus from the dead will also raise us with Jesus and present us with you to himself" (4:14). It is possible that Paul is replying to false teachers in Corinth who did not expect a real, physical resurrection. Paul is anxious to underline that we won't be floating in heaven as disembodied spirits: "we will not be found naked" (5:3). Instead, we will be clothed with our heavenly dwelling (vv. 1–2).

2. We Will No Longer Face the Pains of Our Mortality (5:4)

Paul explains that our fragile tent will be replaced by a permanent building. He now uses another graphic image. Just like a large fish swallowing a smaller one, our mortality will be "swallowed up by life" (5:4). This is a wonderful aspect of the Christian hope. While scientific progress might lengthen our lifespan or improve its quality through hormone therapy or organ replacement, the inevitable limitations of our physical life confront us with increasing intensity as we grow older. But there will come a day, says Paul, when those limitations will be done away with.

Once again Paul is providing us with an important perspective on present suffering. We cannot escape the burdens of our mortal life. But we know that mortality will be swallowed up, and in our new home we will experience the life of the Spirit in all its fullness. This will be the completion of the inward renewal about which Paul wrote in the previous chapter (4:16).

3. We Now Experience Restlessness (5:2, 4)

Twice in these verses Paul refers to the fact that "Meanwhile, we groan" (5:2–4). This language is similar to Paul's wonderful description of the future in Romans 8, where he also states that we, in common with the created world, "groan . . . as we wait eagerly for . . . the redemption of our bodies" (Rom 8:19–23; see also Phil 3:20–21). Until that future day, there is a restlessness we inevitably experience as part of the tension of living in the present world while also being citizens of the world to come. We long for the day when we will be clothed with our new bodies. Such restlessness is part of the evidence of the Spirit's work, as we anticipate that day when there will be no more suffering, no more tears, no more dying.

To underline the absolute certainty of it all, Paul drives home the point with two strong assurances.

4. God Had this in Mind All Along (5:5)

"Now the one who has fashioned us for this very purpose is God" (5:5). The word "God" is emphatic – *God* prepared us for this. If he has begun a good work in us, then he will bring it to completion (Phil 1:6). Our eventual home in heaven is the fulfilment of God's purposes, from which he will not be distracted. Nothing in Paul's experience or ours will deflect him, but his plans will be achieved.

Writing on the subject of hope in his book *The Spirit of Prague*, Ivan Klima sums up how many people see the future: "Because death appears to be the only absolute in human life, all hope is relative, an illusion that helps man make it to the gallows."[2] But Paul's assurances show that death, while real and unavoidable, is not the final curtain which Klima supposes. God's purposes for all those who have trusted Christ extend beyond the defeated enemy of death, in line with his eternal good purposes for his creation.

---

2. Ivan Klima, *The Spirit of Prague* (London: Granta Books, 1994), 81.

5. God Has Given Us a Sign (5:5)

God has given us the Spirit, "guaranteeing what is to come" (5:5). The Holy Spirit is the first instalment of all that will follow in eternity. The presence of the Holy Spirit is God's assurance to us of a sure and certain future. The Spirit's work in our lives now is one of daily renewal (4:16). He empowers us to live our new life, despite the frustrations of our mortal existence. He makes Jesus real to us, despite the distractions of our sinful nature and the world around us. So his work now is a signpost to the future, evidence of God's intention to complete that work of re-creation which the Spirit has already begun.

It is relatively easy for us Christians to speak confidently about the future life, until we ourselves confront death – the death of a friend or close relative, or our own imminent death. At such moments we need to ensure that the strong promises and assurances of this section of Paul's letter live in our hearts as well as our heads. In a moving testimony to the reality of these verses, the British evangelist David Watson wrote about his feelings as he passed through the closing months of his battle with cancer:

> For many years I had been telling people that I am not afraid to die. I know the reality of Christ in my own experience. He has made God real in my life, and has promised one day he will welcome me into his home in heaven. At the same time, I realised that the time had now come to place the whole of my life into God's hands once again, and to renew my trust in him for all that lay ahead of me.[3]

Questions

1. We know that death is the last thing people want to talk about, but why are Christians sometimes also fearful about the subject? How does a passage like this change our emotions, motivations and future perspective?

2. In what ways can you share Paul's sense of restlessness and groaning (5:2–4)?

3. How can we help one another to confront the ageing process, and the inevitability of death, with a greater sense of confidence and security?

---

3. David Watson, *Fear No Evil* (London: Hodder & Stoughton, 1984), 30.

Resurrection

Paul's description of our resurrection bodies in chapter 5 enlarges his earlier teaching recorded in 1 Corinthians 15:25–28.

The idea of resurrection appears in several places in the New Testament. There are some examples of those who were raised from death to life, such as the widow's son (Luke 7:14) and Lazarus (John 11:43–44), but they were raised to mortal life, and would die again. Christians are also described as having been "raised with him," a spiritual resurrection that defines our new life in Christ (Col 2:12).

The pivotal point is Christ's bodily resurrection, the key event which guarantees the resurrection of all who trust in him (1 Cor 6:14). Paul uses the idea of firstfruits to describe this reality: "But Christ has indeed been raised from the dead, the firstfruits of those who have fallen asleep" (1 Cor 15:20; see also 15:23). Since Christ has been raised, a great harvest will follow!

The question naturally arises: what exactly happens when a believer dies before the return of Christ? On the one hand, Paul implies an immediate conscious existence in 2 Corinthians 5:8 and Philippians 1:23: "to depart, and be with Christ." On the other hand, the New Testament also uses the language of sleep, which for some implies some form of "intermediate state" until the Lord returns.

First, it is important to recognize that we are time-bound. To leave this life is to leave the time order, and so we naturally find it difficult to think in other categories. Second, while there are some passages which imply a waiting period (the martyrs in Revelation 6:9–11 are described as waiting and longing for the final fulfilment of God's purposes), others imply that believers who have died will be with Christ when he returns (1 Thess 3:13; 4:14).

The words of Jesus to the dying thief (Luke 23:43) also encourage us to believe that the first conscious moment of the believer after death will be the Lord's coming and the resurrection.

We are not given much information about what our resurrection bodies will be like. Paul teaches in both 1 Corinthians 15:38 and 2 Corinthians 5:1–2 that it is God's work. We know too that it will be a body free from sickness and decay (1 Cor 15:42–43). The resurrection of believers will be part of the renewal of the entire creation, which Paul celebrates in Romans 8:1–25. For now, we eagerly await the return of

Christ who, "by the power that enables him to bring everything under his control, will transform our lowly bodies so that they will be like his glorious body" (Phil 3:20–21).

15

Our Eyes on the Horizon
2 Corinthians 5:6–10

> **Knowing that our future is certain has vital implications for life here and now.**

Whenever the New Testament writers spoke about the future, they invariably drew conclusions for the present. As they encouraged their readers with an eternal perspective, they also demonstrated how such a hope fed back to the present realities of Christian living. Paul is no different, and in this next section he continues to describe the future, but he does so by drawing a series of implications for our lives now.

1. We Live by Faith, Not by Sight (5:6–8)

These verses breathe a spirit of assurance. Paul's certainty about the future dominates his thinking and, despite the pressures he was facing even as he wrote this letter, he could say that "we are always confident" (5:6). He knew he would one day be with Christ. As long as he lived in his body, he would be away from the Lord. So, clearly, he would prefer to move house! He would far rather be with the Lord (vv. 6–8). But to speak in such a way could lead his readers to conclude that he therefore does not know the Lord's presence now. He may be "away from the Lord" as far as his physical existence is concerned, but all Christians enjoy the Lord's fellowship here and now. As he stresses in verse 7, "we live by faith, not by sight." We wait for the day when we will finally be with Christ, but now we live our lives in union with him, having exercised faith in him and his saving gospel.

This simple phrase – "by faith, not by sight" – is very significant in shaping a right attitude to Christian living. Paul is sure about God's good purposes for the future, but he is realistic about his present life. He does not expect everything about the future to be realized now; he knows he will continue to face pressures, to be "burdened" and to "groan" (v. 4). His present life is one characterized by faith both in what God has achieved and in what he will finally achieve in the gospel. He has been saved from the consequences of sin, judgment and death; he is now being saved by God's presence and protection; and he will one day be saved when everything is summed up on the day of Christ. So, he is aware of the fact that more is to come; some things are not yet visible. "We live by faith, not by sight" (5:7).

In emphasizing this present reality, Paul is simply reinforcing the message of a few verses earlier: "We fix our eyes not on what is seen, but on what is unseen" (4:18).

2. We Aim to Please God (5:9)

The future hope which Paul has described is an incentive to us to have one supreme ambition – pleasing God. All other human ambitions must be submitted to this primary goal. We will return to this theme later in 2 Corinthians 5, when Paul draws conclusions in the light of Christ's work on the cross: "He died for all, that those who live should no longer live for themselves but for him" (v. 15).

This is a great encouragement and a great corrective. When we face criticism from others, or when we feel that our best efforts in Christian service are unrecognized or unrewarded, we can take heart that in the end we are answerable to God. We make it our ambition to please Christ, not other people. But it is also a corrective, for there are many times in our lives when our fundamental motivation is our own selfish desire. So, in the light of what Christ has done on the cross, and in the light of what the future holds, it is important to make this verse a filter through which to pass all our ambitions and desires. Anticipating the day when we will be with Christ, we should now make it our goal to please him in all we do.

3. We Are Responsible for How We Live (5:10)

Paul describes one further aspect of the Christian's future. He describes our judgment, and in doing so he builds a bridge between this section of his letter, describing the future, and the next section, where he urges the Corinthians to be active in the ministry of reconciliation. But what is this judgment which we Christians face? Surely we have been saved by Christ and there can be no future condemnation?

The judgment which Paul describes is not a judgment concerning our eternal destiny. Rather, it will be a time for giving an account of how we have lived our lives, a judgment on our stewardship. Paul's teaching in his first letter to the Corinthians (1 Cor 3:11–15) can help us. He writes there of the importance of ensuring that our lives are built on the foundation of Christ. He is the one foundation who will withstand all tests. We are secure if our lives are built on him. But there is more to be said. The question remains: how will we build on that foundation? Will we build with those things which are short-lived – wood, hay, straw – or will we build with those things which are of lasting value – gold, silver, precious stones? One day the quality of our building work will be tested, and on that judgment day, will it survive or will it disappear in a cloud of smoke?

Paul's illustration is similar to the children's story of the wolf and the three little pigs. Each of the pigs builds a house. The first house is made of straw, which the wolf easily blows down. The pig runs to join the second pig, whose house is made of wood. The wolf successfully demolishes this house too, and the two pigs run to the third house, this time made of bricks. Despite his best efforts, the wolf cannot blow the house down. The moral of the children's story is clear: how you build matters. And the point of Paul's teaching is just as direct: how you live your life now will have eternal consequences. Paul refers to the fact that the judgment we will face on that day will be a very practical one, "for the things done while in the body, whether good or bad" (2 Cor 5:10). Everything will be out in the open. That judgment day for Christians is not intended to cloud our hope or dampen our joy at the prospect of being with Christ. Rather, it is there as a stimulus to faithful service, a reminder of our obligation to live for Christ. How do I use my time, my gifts, my resources and my many God-given opportunities? All of these things matter, Paul says, in the light of the future. Will we look back on our lives and see that we have built only things that are temporary, or will we have built something that will last, something for eternity?

Throughout this section Paul has shown that future hope does not make us less committed to the present but motivates us fully to live our lives for God, shaped by the three incentives he has given us. We are to live by faith and not by sight, to please him and not ourselves, and for eternity and not for this world. There is an old Judee Sill folk song called "The Vigilante" which describes in its refrain a perspective of which Paul would have approved: "He's got his eyes on the horizon, and his boots on his feet."[1]

Questions

1. Paul would rather be away from the body and at home with the Lord (5:8). Does this mean that he doesn't really care about this world? How should we balance delight in the prospect of heaven with care for and pleasure in God's world here and now?

2. Is there a place for ambition in the Christian life, such as academic qualifications or success in industry? If so, how does it sit alongside Paul's teaching that we should make it our ambition to please Christ?

3. What practical difference does the thought of future judgment make to your work and behaviour now? In your group, write a few sentences under the heading "Today is my last day."

---

1. https://www.youtube.com/watch?v=E7Uk5ul-tME.

16

Motivation for Ministry
2 Corinthians 5:11–15

> Christian service is governed not by self-interest
> but by very different motives, related to our
> commitment to God and our love for others.

Not long ago I was asked to interview a young graduate for a position in a Christian organization which worked across Europe. I asked him why he was interested in Christian service of this kind. He replied that there were two main reasons: first, to be financially secure, and second, to be able to travel in Europe. Anyone involved in Christian ministry will know that such a comment was not only naive in terms of expectation, but also self-centred in terms of motivation. For all true Christian ministry is costly, as we have seen in this letter. Not only that, for Christians to survive the ups and downs of such work, their fundamental motivation must be clear and well-founded.

In this section, Paul continues to describe the characteristics of his ministry, and he reveals his motivation for service. It is shaped not by self-interest, but by a commitment to serve Christ and his fellow believers.

1. Godly Fear (5:11)

In the light of the previous verse on the sober theme of future judgment, Paul starts this section on the ministry of reconciliation by showing that "to fear the Lord" is an appropriate response (5:11). By this he means not cringing fear but a sense of awe. We are responsible to our Judge, and consequently we have a reason to live our lives as good stewards who will one day have to give an account.

In particular, fear of the Lord should drive us to persuade others of their need for the gospel of reconciliation. We have seen how Paul has frequently expressed his dependence on the Lord ("our competence comes from God," 3:5), and he knows that his ministry is a ministry of the Spirit. Nevertheless, he frequently engaged in persuasion, reason and argument, trusting the Spirit to open the eyes of those to whom he spoke.

Future judgment should provoke within us a sense of godly fear. And godly fear should motivate us to persuade others to turn to Christ and escape the wrath to come.

2. Transparency (5:11–12)

As part of his defence against his critics, Paul has already indicated that he has been transparent, and everything was out in the open (2:1; 4:2). In this section he makes the point once again, stressing that "what we are is plain to God" and also to the Corinthians. His motives are clear. He is not trying to win approval by pretending to be something he isn't. Just as one day the books will be open when he faces judgment (5:10), so now his life is transparent, open for all to read.

Again, he anticipates an objection. He is not boasting (v. 12), but he is trying to correct the perspective of the Corinthians. His critics had a distorted view of how to judge a true apostle, and Paul was trying to counter this. What matters, he says, is the inside, not the outside – a heart that is right with God and is seeking his kingdom, not an outward display of macho heroics or skilful eloquence.

It is never easy for us to be sure about our motives. Self-interest, pride, personal gain – they often pollute our Christian service. The kind of transparency to which Paul refers is an important quality to be nurtured, and the place to begin is God's presence. Then we will be able to say, "what we are is plain to God"; and in turn we can say to others, "I hope it is also plain to your conscience."

3. Concern for Others (5:12–13)

After all that Paul has written so far, the Corinthians must have got the message that Paul's ministry was motivated by a deep concern for their well-being. Not only is he concerned to help them respond to the critics (5:12), he also explains that his attitudes and behaviour have been shaped consistently by a desire to serve them and to bring glory to God (v. 13). There is no trace of self-interest, as he will explain more fully in verse 15.

It is not easy to unravel what Paul is getting at in verse 13, but perhaps some were suggesting that Paul was going crazy. All that hard work and personal suffering: sheer lunacy. Or maybe it was the spiritual experiences and speaking in tongues: the man was seriously unbalanced, they thought. But Paul insists that it is a matter for God to judge. Every aspect of his life, even if judged by others to be extreme, was governed by a desire to serve the Lord and his people.

4. Compelling Love (5:14–15)

Paul now arrives at the fundamental motivation of his life. "The very spring of our actions is the love of Christ" (PHILLIPS). It is Christ's love for Paul which exerts a firm pressure on him, pushing him forward in his service. Paul's logic in these verses is clear. Christ died for me, so I no longer live for myself but live for him: "The love of Christ leaves us no choice" (5:14 NEB).

For Paul, it was not just the thought of Jesus the Judge which motivated his service (vv. 10–11), but Jesus the Saviour, whose self-giving on the cross was the compelling force in his own life, turning him away from self-centred living. The key facts are expressed in these two verses:

- *[Christ] died for all.* He is the Saviour of the world. The scope of his work is universal – all men and women, irrespective of their culture or background, can know salvation through repentance and faith in Christ. He died the death that we deserved.
- *Therefore all died.* All those who have benefited from Christ's saving work have renounced their old way of life. Christ's death for us means death to sin and self, as Paul goes on to state clearly in the next verse. The "all" does not imply that everyone, irrespective of their response to Christ, will benefit from his work. Rather, all who have received him will have died to sin and self.
- *That those who live should no longer live for themselves.* The centre of gravity in our lives is no longer self-interest, but the service of Christ who has given everything for us.
- *But for him who died for them and was raised again.* Paul's language highlights two past historical events – Christ's death and resurrection. We have died to our old way of life, and now live for Christ, because

of the objective reality of Christ's work and because of our union with him.

All Christian service should be empowered by these fundamental motivations. We are responsible to Jesus our Judge; our actions are shaped not by self-interest but by a concern for God's glory and the welfare of others; and we are loved by Jesus our Saviour, who gave himself for us.

Questions

1. When someone criticizes you, what are your initial reactions and responses? Try to be honest! What do these tell you about your motives in Christian service?

2. How can both fear and love motivate us at one and the same time?

3. We persuade people (see 5:11). Note that Paul does not say here, "We preach the gospel to people." What does this tell us about evangelism? What are the implications for us and our churches?

Universalism

"[Christ] died for all" expresses a truth which is found throughout the New Testament. God's purpose of salvation is not limited to one race or nation. His concerns are global.

From the opening pages of the Bible God declares his international concern, promising Abraham that "all peoples on earth will be blessed through you" (Gen 12:3). The prophets predicted that the Servant of the Lord would be a light to the Gentiles, so "that my salvation may reach to the ends of the earth" (Isa 49:6). The psalmists repeated the theme regularly, urging the tiny Hebrew nation to broaden its vision: "Say among the nations, 'The LORD reigns'" (Ps 96:10).

On the basis of his universal authority, Jesus urged his followers to go and "make disciples of all nations" (Matt 28:18–20), and the book of Acts shows that the early Christian preachers, empowered by the Spirit, took that charge seriously as the word of the Lord spread out in ever-widening circles from Jerusalem, out into "all Judea and Samaria, and to the ends of the earth" (Acts 1:8). Paul insisted that the church expressed a similar universality, made up of Jew and Gentile alike (Eph 2:11–22). There would be no room for racial, economic or gender distinctions in this new global family, for "there is neither Jew nor Gentile, neither slave nor free, nor is there male and female, for you are all one in Christ Jesus" (Gal 3:28).

This legitimate universalism has sometimes been pushed beyond its proper biblical limits, and the term "universalism" has also come to describe the belief that all humankind will eventually be saved. The argument includes the suggestion that God, in his love for his creation, will allow an opportunity after death for people to respond to his offer of salvation.

This view, however, cannot be found in the New Testament. Paul himself clearly rejected such a universalism. In 2 Corinthians 2 he has already spoken of "those who are being saved and those who are perishing" (2:15–16), and he used similar language in 1 Corinthians 1:18–24. The same teaching appears in Ephesians 5:4–6 and Philippians 1:28.

The seriousness of sin and the reality of God's judgment are also significant New Testament themes, which make clear that the distinction between the Christian and non-Christian continues after death (John 3:36; Acts 10:42; Rom 2:12–16). Jesus himself makes plain that there is such a thing as the final ruin of those who refuse to believe, and his direct teaching as well as his parables leave us in no doubt that not all will be saved (Matt 12:37–50; 22:11–14; 25:41–46). There are clearly two destinies described in the New Testament: "He will punish those who do not know God and do not obey the gospel of our Lord Jesus. They will be punished with everlasting destruction and shut out from the presence of the Lord" (2 Thess 1:8–9).

As much as we might wish to ignore or remove such teaching from the New Testament, it is part of God's authoritative word that should be neither neglected nor distorted. If it causes us pain to believe and teach it, how much more must the heart of the Creator and Redeemer be broken by such a devastating reality.

We can be sure, however, that heaven will be populated by an innumerable multitude "from every nation, tribe, people and language" (Rev 7:9–12). John's vision of heaven demonstrates that God's international family will be there only because of Christ's work: they are each standing before the throne and "in front of the Lamb." It is his shed blood which makes it possible for that multi-racial, multi-ethnic family to be in heaven.

17

The Ministry of Reconciliation
2 Corinthians 5:16–21

> God's initiative in reconciling us to him through Christ results in wide-ranging changes of attitude, lifestyle, destiny and responsibility.

There are several New Testament pictures which help us to understand Christ's work on the cross. In our day most people identify with the illustration taken from the world of relationships: reconciliation. Whether it is against a background of marriage breakdown, or tensions between parents and children, or fracture between management and the workforce, the idea of being reconciled rings bells for most of us.

The restoration of a relationship with the God who made us is the most fundamental reconciliation of all, and Paul explains how that impacts our lives. He looks at a variety of levels.

1. A New Outlook (5:16)

Paul has already explained that one result of his new life in Christ is that he looks at his own life differently. He no longer lives for himself, but for Christ (5:15). A further consequence ("So from now on," v. 16) is that he now looks at other people differently too. He does not judge them by the standards of this world, whether by external image or by nationality or culture. He has already emphasized that it is what is on the inside that matters (4:16; 5:12). To recognize that Christ died for all (v. 14) will mean that we look at other people with a new perspective.

Before Paul was converted, he judged Jesus by his own religious prejudices. Someone who had been executed on a cross certainly couldn't be the deliverer whom the Jews were expecting. But after he met Christ, Paul's estimate was different. Christ was not some obscure Galilean who had died a shameful and humiliating death. He was the Saviour of the world.

To be in God's family is to see people differently. We refuse to judge people by the world's yardstick, or the prejudices of our own culture. Instead, we see each person as someone for whom Christ died.

2. A New Creation (5:17)

In one of the best-known descriptions of Christian conversion, in 5:17 Paul describes the change which comes about when we come to faith in Christ.

- *It is universal*: "if anyone is in Christ." Paul indicates once again that reconciliation is open to all, since Christ died for all (v. 14).
- *It is total*: there is "a new creation." As Paul tries to express the change which occurs, he could not have chosen a more profound illustration. Becoming a Christian means we enter a whole new world of experience. It is a total transformation, a new creation.
- *It is radical*: "the old has gone, the new has come." Reconciliation with God means a radical change of allegiance. Our old way of life is to be put to death, and our new life in Christ is to be the dominant characteristic of all that we are and all that we do.

One of the greatest challenges in Christian mission in many countries is referred to as "nominalism": people who call themselves Christians (up to 96 percent of the population in some countries), but who do not have genuine faith in Christ and do not live a life of committed discipleship. According to Paul's teaching here, to be a Christian is not just to believe in a creed, or undergo Christian ceremonies, or adopt a Christian code of behaviour. Christianity is Christ, and a Christian is a person united to him, transformed by him and living for him.

3. A New Relationship (5:18–19, 21)

Here is the heart of Paul's description of reconciliation. Sin has created the barrier between us and God. This produces the sense of alienation between a holy God and rebellious people. We are cut off from God by our sin, and God is cut off from us by his holy rejection of sin. There is nothing which we can do to restore the relationship unless God intervenes. So Paul explains first of all that God has taken the initiative: "All this is from God" (5:18).

Through Christ, Paul explains, the barrier is removed. God no longer counts our sins against us (v. 19) because Christ has taken them away. Christ's death was no accident but was the culmination of his ministry and the purpose of his mission. It was the means by which our sin could be removed. Jesus took our sin on himself when he died on the cross, and it was such a complete identification that Paul uses the phrase "God made him who had no sin to be sin for us" (v. 21). In these verses Paul describes what has come to be known as the doctrine of the "great exchange." God takes our sin and in turn gives us Christ's righteousness (v. 21).

This is the foundation for the new relationship which is possible for everyone who turns to Christ. Because of the cross, our sin has been blotted out, and God's holy anger has been taken away. Christ has taken the judgment which we deserved, and has brought us home, reconciling us to God through the profound mystery of his death.

4. A New Ministry (5:20)

Paul now explains what this means in terms of Christian ministry. Having been reconciled, he is now a minister of reconciliation. He uses the illustration of the ambassador, the king's envoy. It is a bold analogy. As Paul implies, we are speaking on behalf of God. It is "as though God were making his appeal through us" (5:20). We are speaking "on Christ's behalf" (v. 20).

It is not uncommon these days, in a world of other religions, for Christians to be asked why they are so arrogant as to claim that the gospel is for every culture. What gives them the right? These verses help us respond with conviction to such a question. Christians are called to proclaim that "Christ died for all" (v. 14), and the basis of their authority is that they speak "on Christ's behalf" (v. 20). Of course, this must be done with humility and with sensitivity to the culture in which we live, but we should never shrink from the task of Christian proclamation or be intimidated by today's religious pluralism. The ministry of reconciliation is founded on the fact that we are sent as ambassadors by the King.

But the verse continues with the word "implore." The appeal we make to others to be reconciled is made not with impersonal detachment but with a sense of urgency and passion. Paul may be an ambassador, but he does not stand on his dignity. He is on his knees, begging people to be reconciled.

The ministry of reconciliation, then, has both authority and urgency: we implore on Christ's behalf. Since Christ died for all, our task is to take that good news to a world broken by sin, and to do so with the wholehearted commitment of those through whom God has chosen to make his appeal.

Questions

1. What difference will it make to the way we treat people if we see them through the eyes of Jesus on the cross? How does this relate to being "ambassadors for Christ"?

2. Try to describe to a non-Christian friend what God achieved on the cross, using as little Christian "jargon" as possible.

3. How can we proclaim the gospel with authority and passion without frightening people away?

Atonement

"Atonement" refers to the way in which sin is removed from God's sight. It is the foundation for forgiveness. One of the most profound descriptions of Christ's death in 2 Corinthians 5 is "God made him . . . to be sin for us" (v. 21). Almost shocking in its intensity, the thought behind Paul's writing is that God substituted the Lord Jesus for the sinners who deserved his judgment.

Paul also shows that substitution implies exchange: if the sinless Jesus took our sin, in him we "become the righteousness of God" (v. 21). Paul uses a number of word pictures to explain Christ's death. "Justification" is a word taken from the law courts, and "propitiation" is from the temple.

"Justification" is a word picture which begins with the fact that we stand guilty and condemned before the Judge of all the earth. It is only by his gracious initiative that he declares, first, that we are acquitted, and second, that we are declared righteous. The word "justify" means exactly this: to count as righteous. (See Rom 3:21–23; 4:23–25; Gal 2:15–16.)

This is not the same as amnesty, which would overlook our sinfulness. It is God's act of justice because of one essential aspect in God's solution to our dilemma – someone else stands in our place.

Christ is our substitute, standing where we are, in our guilty state, and he takes upon himself all that was due to us because of our sin. He has taken the penalty for our law-breaking. So, Paul writes to the Romans, "While we were still sinners, Christ died for us. Since we have now been justified by his blood . . ." (Rom 5:8–9).

This is the great exchange to which Paul refers in 2 Corinthians 5. Christ's acceptability before God, his righteousness, is counted as if it were ours. And our unacceptability, our unrighteousness, is counted as if it were his. As Isaiah prophesied, "The Lord has laid on him the iniquity of us all" (Isa 53:6).

This is filled out by Paul with another word picture, this time taken from the temple: "propitiation." This is the word which describes Jesus's sacrifice on the cross as the only means by which guilty sinners could be delivered from God's wrath. In Romans Paul writes that "God presented Christ as a sacrifice of atonement" (Rom 3:25). Paul had earlier mounted heavy artillery in Romans 1 to show that all men and women are subject to God's wrath. For sin is more than guilt; it is a wrong relationship with God, which is double-sided. We are alienated from God by sin, and God is alienated from us by wrath.

It is for this reason that the law court imagery by itself is insufficient to convey the full meaning of Christ's atoning work. God is not an uninterested party, as a judge in the courts is likely to be. He is offended. And Paul explains that Jesus faced the full force of God's wrath when dying on the cross. This is not some third party because it was God himself in the person of his Son who made the sacrifice of atonement, as we have seen here in 2 Corinthians 5:21.

In this way, God's dilemma was solved. He remains just, by judging sin, and at the same time shows his redeeming love to guilty sinners by taking that penalty himself. As Paul expressed it in Romans, God's justice was demonstrated "so as to be just and the one who justifies those who have faith in Jesus" (Rom 3:26). It is this truth, in all of its profound mystery, which led John to declare, "This is love . . . that he . . . sent his Son as an atoning sacrifice [propitiation] for our sins" (1 John 4:10). It is the greatest expression of love this world will ever know.

18

Consistent Behaviour
2 Corinthians 6:1–13

Paul explains that in all circumstances he has tried to live as the gospel demands.

Perhaps second only to politicians, Christian leaders who fall from grace are the special target of popular newspapers and social media attacks. Whether it is a church minister who has run off with his secretary, or a treasurer who has embezzled church funds, the papers seem to take a malicious delight in exposing such failures. Stories like this sell because they are blatant examples of hypocrisy. There is a salacious side too, but there is an understandable reaction when people sniff religious pretence, or sense double standards in Christian leaders or politicians who claim the right to tell everyone else how to live. Behaving consistently really matters.

If we share in the ministry of reconciliation, acting as ambassadors for the King, then we, too, will want to ensure that we live lives of absolute integrity. We may not all be officers in the church, but if we are true believers, then we are called to be servants of Christ, ministers of the new covenant (as we have seen in 2 Corinthians 3). How we behave, particularly when we are under pressure, is an important part of our Christian witness.

1. Now Is the Time to Act (6:1–2)

Having explained in the last chapter the good news of God's reconciling grace, Paul now points out one of the greatest dangers the Corinthians faced: "to receive God's grace in vain" (6:1). It is always a temptation for Christians to sit back in the comfort of their own security, and to fail to take the responsibility to live as the gospel demands.

Paul urges the Corinthians to act, appealing to them as God's fellow workers so as to underline the seriousness of his request. Quoting from Isaiah 49:8, he reminds them that the day of grace is today, not tomorrow. There is no time to waste. This is not an evangelistic appeal, urging them to be saved, but rather an appeal to the Corinthians to live by the gospel. They should not throw away the present opportunity or be distracted by sin and live a life that is inconsistent with God's grace.

To receive God's grace in vain means that our practice does not match up with what we say we believe. Our lives are a denial of the implications of the gospel. In such circumstances our Christian lives become stale and barren, and our witness is powerless and ineffective.

2. Building Bridges, Not Road-Blocks (6:3)

Paul explains in this next section how, in a variety of circumstances, he has sought to carry out his apostolic ministry. He is deeply concerned that his ministry should "not be discredited," a word which conveys the idea of mocking and ridicule (6:3). He is determined that there should be nothing in his life which would be a "stumbling-block" to others, holding them back from faith in the gospel or from progress in their discipleship (v. 3). It would be deeply disturbing if someone failed to become a Christian not because of the offence of the cross, but because of our inconsistent behaviour. Rather, our lives should so complement the truth of the gospel that our witness is enhanced, and people are drawn closer to Christ.

3. Commending Ourselves in Every Way (6:4–10)

Paul describes how his life matched his profession in a range of tough situations, which he now lists in one of several "catalogues" that appear in his letter. In chapter 4 he listed some of his hardships, and a more extensive catalogue appears in chapter 11. He begins this list with three groups of three trials, each of which he faced with "great endurance" (6:4), and his purpose is to demonstrate the genuine integrity of his ministry.

The first three pressures are described in general terms: "troubles, hardships and distresses" (v. 4). Then he describes three specific pressures inflicted by others: "beatings, imprisonments and riots" (v. 5). And finally, three which were self-imposed: "hard work, sleepless nights and hunger" (v. 5). In these ways, he commends his ministry. As we shall see in the final chapters of the letter, Paul does not want to be guilty of the boasting which characterized his opponents in Corinth. They apparently took pride in physical appearance and in heroic achievements. As far as Paul is concerned, if he had to boast he would boast about his weaknesses (11:30). And here in chapter 6 he indicates that the best way of judging the integrity of his ministry is to watch how he responded to pressures of every kind. It is by patient endurance, coupled with consistent behaviour, that he wishes to commend his ministry.

The next set of nine expressions (6:6–7) describe the qualities with which he sought to carry out his work. They are each the result of the Holy Spirit's ministry, for he is the one who produces the harvest of qualities which Paul lists. And again, they underline that here is a man whose ministry is consistent. To paraphrase verse 7, "Our sole defence . . . is a life of integrity" (PHILLIPS).

Paul's final cluster of nine is a series of contrasts (vv. 8–10), illustrating the stresses and strains which characterized his ministry. Whether people praised him or mocked him, whether they welcomed him or rejected him, whatever the circumstances of his life, Paul has gained God's perspective. His value system is shaped by the values of the kingdom, not the values of this world.

It is very easy for our lives to be controlled by our circumstances, or by the expectations of others around us. In a world which thinks negatively about the Christian faith, we can easily be tempted to compromise our faith or dilute our Christian witness. Paul teaches us in these verses that we need to hold the things of this world lightly. If we are concerned with our own reputation or honour, with material comfort and security, then it is unlikely that we will live a life worthy of the gospel. Our ministry will be "discredited," and instead of encouraging others forward, we will be placing a roadblock across their path. But true servants of God, filled with his Spirit, will want to live a life which is consistent with the gospel they proclaim.

4. Open Hearts (6:11–13)

These verses provide further evidence of Paul's honesty and openness with the Corinthian believers (4:2; 5:11–12). He has taken them into his trust, exposing his frailties and vulnerabilities, as he has described the hardships of his service for them and for the Lord: "We have spoken freely to you, Corinthians" (6:11).

Using their name in this verse heightens the sense of emotional intensity. He has opened his heart to them, and longs that they should do the same towards him (v. 13). Much of this letter reveals Paul's pastoral heart, and his deep affection for the believers who were being seduced by the rival teachers who had arrived in Corinth. There are few things which are more painful than love spurned, and this is how Paul felt: he was expressing his affection towards them, openly describing his thoughts and feelings, yet they seemed cold and indifferent (v. 12). He will pick up the appeal again in chapter 7, but as a father speaking to his children (v. 13), he appeals to them to open wide their hearts to him. In the light of the pastoral discipline about which he will shortly speak, an open and loving relationship will be essential if Paul's message is to be received and acted upon.

Genuine Christian fellowship in our churches will be open-hearted. We can usually tell that this is a feature of church life by such practical signs as open homes, not formal relationships; open fellowship, not special in-groups; open communication, which confronts as well as encourages, not innuendo and gossip. Opening our hearts wide is an essential part of Christian integrity, and it represents an attractive feature of Christian community, which commends the gospel in an age of broken relationships.

Questions

1. Paul speaks about receiving the grace of God in vain (6:1). Are there areas of your life where you feel this might be the case? What do you think Paul is getting at, and how can we make sure that we avoid this?

2. In what ways might the work of the church be in danger of being discredited, in the sense that Paul is describing, and how can that be avoided?

3. Read through Paul's lists once again (6:4–10), pausing to reflect on your own life, and whether you are commending the gospel in the various situations Paul is describing.

4. How can we create an "open heart" kind of fellowship in our churches?

5. Take time to pray for the many Christians around the world who are experiencing the kinds of hardship to which Paul refers in this passage.

19

No Compromise
2 Corinthians 6:14–7:1

> **God's people must live distinctive lives if they are to reflect his character and honour his name.**

At first sight this next section appears to be a sudden digression from Paul's theme. He has been describing the features of his own ministry and has made an appeal to the Corinthians to open their hearts towards him (6:13), an appeal he will repeat within a few more verses (7:2).

The present section is a call to holiness, and it is not immediately clear why Paul introduces it. But the theme of distinctiveness in Christian living certainly connects to the concern for consistent ministry with which Paul began the chapter. He did not want Christian ministry to be discredited (6:2), so the encouragement to the Corinthians to live pure, uncontaminated lives (7:1) makes good sense.

1. Pulling in Different Directions (6:14–16)

Paul begins with a call not to be "yoked together with unbelievers" (6:14), a picture borrowed from the book of Deuteronomy (22:10). There the law forbids ploughing a field using different kinds of animals working together. An ox and a donkey would pull at different speeds and would therefore be ineffective when harnessed together. And this was one example of several instances in Old Testament law where God's people were required to act consistently. Just as there should be no mismatch when it comes to ploughing a field, so there should be no mixing of crops in the field, no mixing of different fibres in their home-spun cloth (see Lev 19:19) and, for the people themselves, no contamination by their pagan neighbours (see Lev 18:24–30). It reflected God's concern that his people should be set apart, living their lives by his standards.

Paul urges the Corinthians to live in this distinct, undivided way, and to press home the point, he asks a series of five rhetorical questions (2 Cor 6:14–16). Each question shows that trying to combine secular and Christian values is like trying to mix oil and water – it will not work. Paul again reinforces his case with another well-known Old Testament theme, using a phrase which was common to God's covenant promise: "I will be their God, and they will be my people" (v. 16). How can you belong to God and at the same time flirt with the world? This is part of Paul's continuing concern that the Corinthians should resist the temptation to adopt the false values of the new teachers in town. Consistent believers would not give space in their homes to idols; they would reject any such secular intrusion because their lives and their Christian community are the home of the living God.

Paul takes still more ammunition from his Old Testament arsenal with the strong call to holiness from the prophets: "Come out from them and be separate" (v. 17; see also Isa 52:11). Since these verses have sometimes been misused, it is important to understand that Paul is not arguing for a withdrawal from the world. After all, he has spoken in chapter 5 of the calling to be ambassadors who are sent into the world. We don't automatically call the players off the field when they become members of God's family. We are given the responsibility to live distinctly Christian lives, proclaiming the gospel of reconciliation in the midst of a fallen world. But Paul is urging us to keep our "saltiness" (see Matt 5:14), not to take on the values and ambitions of the secular world.

2. No Compromise (6:15, 17)

This passage (2 Cor 6:14–7:1) has frequently been used to explain why Christians should avoid inappropriate partnerships – not being unequally yoked, for example, in marriage or in business. And this seems a legitimate application of the principles Paul is writing about. If becoming a Christian means your whole view of life changes – different values, different ambitions, different ethical standards and, most importantly, a different authority in your life – how can you share your life intimately with someone outside of God's family? How can you be "at one"? Or as Paul expresses it in verse 15, "What does a believer have in common with an unbeliever?" Painful as it might be initially, the Christian is called to avoid any close liaison which will compromise the distinctness of their calling.

3. Godly Motivation (6:18–7:1)

What is at stake for the Corinthians, and for all of us who are members of God's family (v. 18), is not simply the integrity of our witness but our reverence for God himself. How we behave will reflect on our Father (6:18). We are called to purify ourselves "out of reverence for God" (7:1). The way Paul makes his appeal implies that this is our regular, day-by-day responsibility. There are many things which will drag us away from God's standards, many things which contaminate body and spirit, but we must be committed to the long haul of perfecting holiness (7:1) in a wholehearted way. Nothing should be allowed to infect our minds, hearts or bodies; it is a position of no compromise, of absolute integrity.

At first, Paul's teaching seems unattainable. It seems unrealistic. But notice the way in which his strong call to distinct, holy living is surrounded by warm expressions concerning God's presence. In 6:16 he has said that we are God's dwelling place, his home; he repeats that with the expression "I will live with them and walk among them" (v. 16). Then he assures us that we belong to a God who says, "I will be a Father to you, and you will be my sons and daughters" (v. 18). The calling to live our lives in conformity with God's standards is accompanied by the promise of his empowering presence and compassionate care.

Paul's teaching might have been aimed at the subtle infiltration of secular values into the Corinthian church, introduced by the false teachers about whom Paul is writing so frequently. But his teaching in these verses could not be more relevant to today's church. We face the constant temptation to compromise with the world. Its seductive appeal comes in many forms, and whether it is in the sphere of relationships, business, sexuality, materialism, ambition or lifestyle, we are under constant pressure to conform. But as God's temple, and as God's children, we should challenge the world, not conform to it. That's the kind of Christianity the world needs to see.

Questions

1. What are the most common temptations to compromise that you face? How do you overcome them?

2. Collect all the ways in which Paul pictures our relationship with God in this passage. How do they make a difference to your commitment to live a holy life?

3. As you look at our own culture, in what ways should Christian distinctness or difference be most evident in your life or your church?

20

A Deep Personal Involvement
2 Corinthians 7:2–5

> Being part of the Christian family means we are bound together closely with other believers, but this can sometimes be painful as well as joyful.

Bringing up children is an experience of mixed emotions. It should mostly be joyful, for children are a wonderful gift from God, and their growth and development are fascinating to watch and to experience. But all good parents will know the sorrows associated with discipline. It is an essential element in the formation of children, shaping their character, defining appropriate social behaviours and strengthening their unique gifts and personalities. These are long-term goals; the short-term experience can be painful for parent and child alike.

Paul knew a good deal about such pain. While not having children of his own in a biological family, he expressed extraordinary fatherly concern for those who had come to faith through his ministry. He felt the joys and the sorrows of caring for them, watching over their development, seeing them fail and working to restore them. We have already seen Paul expose his feelings earlier in the letter: "For I wrote to you out of great distress and anguish of heart and with many tears, not to grieve you but to let you know the depth of my love for you" (2:4). Now, in chapter 7, Paul is returning to the problem which he had introduced in chapter 2. He has taken a major detour, describing what constitutes true Christian service, and now he returns to the theme which had caused him so much heartache: failure within the church.

As we saw in chapter 2, there had been a serious failure at Corinth which had grieved Paul, but which had also impacted the whole church. Paul was concerned that appropriate discipline be exercised, but apparently the church had ignored the problem, failing to address the matter adequately. It was this which had provoked Paul's sharp letter of rebuke, the so-called "severe" letter. It was followed by Paul sending Titus to visit the church to ensure they had acted on his advice. The whole episode was deeply painful for Paul. He loved them, and now his relationship with them was strained and uncertain.

When he arrived in Macedonia (7:5), he was concerned that his strong letter might have pushed the Corinthians too far. Maybe he had blown it. Perhaps his tough words had broken the relationship with the Corinthians, and his leadership role was now jeopardized. It wasn't simply the problem of appropriate discipline for the offender in the church. It was closely related to the Corinthians' commitment to Paul as an apostle. The church was dangerously vulnerable if they were close to rejecting Paul's authority. They were in danger of turning their backs on the gospel itself. So these verses tell us much about the demands of Christian relationships.

1. Open Relationships (7:2–4)

In 7:2 Paul repeats the appeal of 6:11: "make room for us in your hearts." He clearly felt they had slammed the door. Verse 2 hints at some of the accusations that were being made against Paul, to which he now replies. With his own characteristic transparency, he confronts these charges with complete honesty. He has not been guilty of acting unjustly or of taking advantage of them. His motives in writing as he did were entirely pure: he longs to have a restored relationship with them, for they are in his heart. They matter to him more than life itself (7:3).

It is not uncommon for Christians to have closed hearts towards each other. There can be a coldness, a defensiveness, which prevents open fellowship. Sometimes it is the result of inappropriate gossip. The false teachers in Corinth were spreading false rumours about Paul, trying to discredit him, and this kind of criticism is sadly typical in many of our own congregations. Malicious gossip is a destructive feature of church life; people who have been injured in some way, or who feel neglected, become embittered and resentful, finding ammunition with which to attack people (often the leaders) within their own Christian community. This not only polarizes a fellowship and paralyses its witness, but most seriously, it dishonours the name of Christ.

Alongside Paul's transparency in defending his behaviour, he also expresses another quality which is essential in all Christian relationships: loyalty. The Corinthians matter deeply to him, and his committed friendship will last (vv. 3–4). So, for our churches: we are redeemed by the same Lord Jesus, we belong to the same Father, we are indwelt by the same Holy Spirit. There should be no room for ugly division or painful fragmentation. We who believe the gospel of reconciliation should be the first to demonstrate its truth in open relationships with one another.

2. Painful Discipline (7:5)

This section also shows us something of the anguish Paul experienced in his parental care for the Corinthians. We have seen in 2:12–13 that he was so distressed by the emotional impact of the disciplinary crisis at Corinth that he couldn't concentrate on anything else, not even his missionary work. He had opportunities to work in Troas, but he was distracted and restless (2:12–13). He was hoping for news from Titus, following his visit to Corinth, but he had still not returned, and Paul felt continued anxiety as he waited in Macedonia (7:5). He faced all kinds of pressures there too: "conflicts on the outside, fears within" (v. 5).

It's impossible to read verse 5 without feeling the emotion. Paul was exercising brave leadership. Godly discipline was necessary, but it clearly took its toll of Paul. Such discipline is always demanding and therefore it is always tempting to avoid it. It would be easy to duck the issue. We would find it more comfortable to ignore a relational breakdown in the Christian community, in the hope that the problem might go away. But that would be a fatal mistake. Like going to the dentist, it is sometimes necessary for a little pain to be inflicted in order to avoid a great deal of pain later. In church life there is no avoiding such discipline, and handled wisely, the outcome will be a depth of maturity in our Christian service and a restoration of relationships that will bring honour to the Lord and healing in the Christian community.

Questions

1. Paul was deeply concerned about the breach of unity between himself and the Corinthians. What are the most common causes of broken fellowship in the Christian community? How does Paul's attitude in this section provide an example we should follow?

2. Why is church unity so important? Read Ephesians 4:1–6 and think about the core reasons Paul gives for living together in unity, discussing why this matters so much.

21

The Right Kind of Sorrow

2 Corinthians 7:6–16

> There are two kinds of repentance, each of which has very different consequences.

Without the benefit of modern communication devices, Paul had to wait for weeks until Titus finally brought him news of how his letter had been received by the Corinthians. And it was the message he had hoped for. They had accepted the letter and had reaffirmed their acceptance of Paul too. Instead of reacting with bitterness, they had responded with genuine sorrow (7:7). He describes the sense of relief and comfort he felt when he received the news from Titus. God comforts the downcast, and Paul experienced that yet again (v. 7; see also 1:4).

1. True Repentance (7:10–11)

The key to understanding the response of the Corinthians is found in 7:10. It summarizes the two ways in which they might have responded, and it provides an important contrast for us to reflect on. There is either "godly sorrow" or "worldly sorrow," and in the verses which follow, Paul demonstrates the significant differences between these two responses.

"Worldly sorrow" is the sorrow of being found out. It is self-centred sorrow. Perhaps we have met a Christian who has done something wrong, admits to failure and even expresses regret: but underneath you can detect the anger and bitterness, even a continuing rebellion. The person has been exposed; pride is wounded. When worldly sorrow sets in, it doesn't lead to genuine repentance or restoration, but quite the reverse. Sourness and resentment can destroy people. In other words, Paul says, it leads to death (v. 10).

"Godly sorrow" is entirely different. It could be literally translated "according-to-God sorrow." The focus of such sorrow is not my wounded pride, but the God whom I have offended. Expressing such sorrow means facing up to failure in God's presence, and it leads to repentance. Unlike worldly sorrow, which breeds frustration and resentment, godly sorrow is the way to restoration, and it "leaves no regret" (v. 10). It is because of the fruitful outcome of godly sorrow that we look back on it with no sense of resentment.

I received a letter not long ago from someone who had faced discipline for certain relational failures. It was a letter of self-pity and self-justification, a letter which shifted blame elsewhere. By contrast, I well remember an example of godly sorrow in the church where I grew up as a child. One of our leaders was found to have been guilty of a specific failure and was disciplined appropriately. But in due course he returned with a new humility and a willingness to serve those whom he had injured. As a young Christian I viewed this man not as a failure but as someone I respected deeply. And this of course is the gospel at work – God's grace in response to those who repent with godly sorrow.

This was precisely how the Corinthians had responded. There was a deep seriousness, a godly grief with repentance, which had opened the door to restoration. Although Paul might have regretted the possible injury he could have caused, or the pain he had inflicted, he now realized that it had been necessary and worthwhile (vv. 8–9). The result had been godly sorrow – with all of its fruitful results – and therefore they had been not harmed but healed by Paul's pastoral intervention.

The result of genuine sorrow is described in verse 11. They didn't point the finger of blame elsewhere; they didn't dismiss the sinful behaviour of the church member concerned or ignore Paul's urgent call for discipline. They clearly took the issue seriously, wanting justice to be carried out; and Paul says they are now innocent in the matter (v. 11).

2. Warm Fellowship (7:6–16)

Reading chapter 7 is an emotional roller-coaster ride. It ranges from deep pain, to restless anxiety, to godly grief, to overwhelming joy. Although Paul has had to introduce stern discipline, he also affirms his confidence in them (v. 4).

Indeed, the chapter closes with a significant feature of Paul's response from which we can learn a great deal. He was ready to confront the Corinthians directly, but didn't criticize them in front of others – not even to Titus, whom he commissioned as the messenger. How did he describe the Corinthians? There was no sense of bitterness or criticism, but rather expressions of pride and confidence in them: "I had boasted to him about you, and you have not embarrassed me. But just as everything we said to you was true, so our boasting about you to Titus has proved to be true as well. . . . I am glad that I can have complete confidence in you" (vv. 14, 16).

One of the most destructive habits in local church life is the tendency, in any situation of conflict, to go to third parties instead of going to the person who has caused the injury. Jesus gave clear guidelines in Matthew 18:15–17 designed to help us handle conflict, and he deliberately emphasized the pattern to follow: go first to the person who has wronged you. But often we will go to others first, seeking sympathy for ourselves and simultaneously criticizing a fellow Christian.

Although Paul had the opportunity to denigrate the Corinthians' character as he briefed Titus, he refused to follow that route. He boasted of his confidence in them. And Paul's pastoral style is seen in this chapter to include the vital ministry of encouragement. Since they had responded with godly sorrow (2 Cor 7:11), he is strong in his affirmations of them, positive about their fellowship and open about his depth of joy.

"I take great pride in you. I am greatly encouraged" (v. 4); "my joy was greater than ever" (v. 7); "by all this we are encouraged" (v. 13); "I am glad I can have complete confidence in you" (v. 16). And Titus was caught up in the same spirit of affirmation and joy. Initially fearful of meeting the Corinthians, he had been warmly received and his own spirit had been refreshed through the visit (vv. 13–15).

Paul's sense of joy didn't come from having scored the points and won the battle. It was the joy of fellowship restored, the triumph of the gospel of grace and reconciliation. The Christian church needs to learn some of the lessons of this chapter, for relational failure is a universal problem within our communities. But the power of the gospel is the same today as it was in the past, and the wise application of such Scriptures as these, in the power of the Spirit, can have the same healing effects as those over which Paul rejoiced in the first century.

Questions

1. Can you think of examples in your own life where you have expressed worldly sorrow rather than godly sorrow? What did the experience feel like? How can we ensure that we react with godly sorrow when facing personal failure?

2. Paul was able to affirm other Christians, even boasting about them to others. Why do we tend to be critical of others rather than affirming? How can we change that attitude?

3. Why is it so difficult to speak directly to a person who has upset us, and so easy to discuss the matter with others rather than with the person concerned? Suggest steps that might help with the problem.

Section 3

Paul Appeals for Generosity

2 Corinthians 8:1–9:15

22

Triangular Giving
2 Corinthians 8:1–5

As he introduces the importance of generous giving, Paul provides a significant example of believers who demonstrated a sacrificial commitment to the Lord and to others.

It doesn't matter whether you're rich or poor, as long as you've got money," professional boxer Joe Lewis once quipped, and that's how many of us feel about the subject. We all have to live in this world; we all have to make ends meet. So surely the matter of money is fairly neutral? In fact, the issue of our use of money is right at the heart of our Christian discipleship. Paul devotes two full chapters to the subject because other significant themes are attached to the matter of giving. They include our understanding of God's grace in the gospel, the implications of fellowship, fundamental motivation in Christian living and even the nature of Christian worship.

Paul has returned to the theme of the collection, having appealed to the Corinthians to contribute when he wrote his first letter (1 Cor 16:1). This offering was for the special needs of the believers in Jerusalem. The church there was under considerable financial pressure and Paul was anxious that a collection be taken from around the region, not only to meet the needs of the Christians in Jerusalem but also as an expression of solidarity between Jewish and Gentile believers. Such practical action would be a clear signal of the unity of believers from different cultural backgrounds.

It seems that the collection had gone well in a number of cities. Corinth had begun well (2 Cor 8:10), but the collection had not been completed. It could have been that they were distracted by internal problems, or perhaps the false teachers had dissuaded them from pursuing the offering as part of their campaign to discredit Paul. Whatever the reasons, since Paul was preparing for his next visit to Corinth, he decided to reinforce his appeal that they complete the offering. Having received the good news from Titus that the Corinthians had expressed their loyalty towards him (7:7), now was the time to press the point once again.

Rather than begin with a direct exhortation to give, Paul introduces the subject with the example of the Macedonian believers. These were churches such as Philippi, Thessalonica and Berea (see Acts 16:9–12; 17:1–15), and the giving of these churches was exemplary. Strong examples can be a powerful incentive to give, sometimes because we are inspired by the actions of others, and sometimes because of a degree of competitiveness. Was this part of Paul's strategy? The sophisticated Corinthians would surely not wish to be outshone by other churches! But it was a fine example to choose, for the Macedonian believers excelled when it came to giving. Paul identifies several significant features of their generosity.

1. Their Giving Was Spiritual (8:1, 5)

This might come as a surprise to those of us used to talking about money simply as a transaction, a means to an end. But generous giving is the result of God's grace working in our lives. Notice how frequently Paul makes reference to this: "the grace that God has given the Macedonian churches" (8:1); "this act of grace" (v. 6); "this grace of giving" (v. 7); "the grace of our Lord Jesus Christ" (v. 9). (See also 9:8, 14.)

It is made more explicit when Paul explains that the Macedonian response was the result of giving themselves "first of all to the Lord" (8:5). Their financial generosity arose from their wholehearted commitment to the lordship of Christ. Everything was surrendered to him. True Christian giving is triangular: we give first to the Lord, then for something or someone. To see giving in this way removes any sense of manipulation on the part of the giver ("Now I have some influence over this project"), and also removes any sense of embarrassment or indebtedness on the part of the receiver. We are giving to God, as part of the total stewardship and worship of our lives. It is this which is in keeping with God's will (v. 5).

2. Their Giving Was Sacrificial (8:2–3)

It must have been God's grace at work, because the Macedonian Christians gave when they could ill afford to do so. They too were under pressure of persecution, and Paul says they suffered from extreme poverty (8:2). Yet despite these constraints, their sacrificial giving was characterized by two qualities. First, it was generous. Paul calls it "rich generosity" (v. 2), and in the next chapter he reminds the Corinthians that this is the kind of giving God looks for. They gave well beyond their means. Second, it was willing (v. 3). There was no need for Paul to urge them to give – indeed, he seems to have been reluctant to make any appeal to them because of their poverty, and the Macedonians pleaded with him to be allowed to make their contribution. Paul will repeat these themes later (9:7).

3. Their Giving Expressed Solidarity (8:4–5)

Their giving was also motivated by a concern for the well-being of other Christians, a desire to have "the privilege of sharing in this service to the Lord's people" (8:4). This is doubly impressive when we know that they themselves faced extreme poverty. But their sense of solidarity with their fellow believers in the body of Christ provoked them to give to the needs of others. Such unselfishness is a mark of true fellowship.

It would be true to say that if Christians today followed the example of the Macedonian believers, the frequency of appeal letters and gift days would be dramatically reduced. It is not easy for us to get inside the skin of these Macedonians, but were we to identify with their needs, we would be even more moved by their generosity. No wonder Paul chose them to introduce his call to the Corinthians – and to us – to be sacrificial in our response to God's grace.

Questions

1. Fund-raising has a rather bad name in Christian circles. How can raising money for a Christian project become a joyful and positive experience?

2. What difference does it make to your giving if you come to see it as "triangular" – giving first to the Lord and then to others?

3. Can you think of examples of sacrificial giving which have inspired you or your group to more generous giving?

The Collection

The collection for the Jerusalem church dominates chapters 8 and 9 of 2 Corinthians. The story probably began when Paul was asked by the Jerusalem leaders not to forget the needs of the poor (Gal 2:10). He then introduced the project, partly because of the urgent need to provide for Christians facing acute shortages, and partly because it was an ideal opportunity to encourage a sense of solidarity between believers from Gentile and Jewish backgrounds.

The poverty of the church in Jerusalem was the result of a cluster of factors. As converted Jews they faced the hostility of their families and neighbours, and probably many lost employment as a result. It is likely that those in work had only menial jobs, hardly securing enough income to cover the needs of their families, let alone the wider Christian community in the city, and we know (Acts 11:27–30) that they also suffered from a famine which added considerably to the sense of deprivation.

Paul refers to the collection in 1 Corinthians 16:1–4, where he gives instructions to the Corinthians to set aside gifts on a regular basis. He had said the same to the Galatian churches. He also refers to those who contributed to the collection in Romans 15:25–28.

As we see from 2 Corinthians 8–9, Paul appealed to the Corinthian church to give generously because this represented an important expression of the grace of the gospel. It would relieve the pressure on needy Christians and would be an important expression of true fellowship. In the early days of the church, it was important to establish the fact that Jewish and Gentile believers were members of the same family, with a commitment to one another that was expressed in practical ways. Some people also think the collection was an expression of thanksgiving by Gentile churches for the special inheritance they had received through their Jewish colleagues. Maybe some of the prophecies of Isaiah and Micah were in their minds, where the prophets predicted that Gentiles would bring gifts to Jerusalem in the last days (Isa 2:2–4; 60:60–61; Mic 4:13).

Paul's energetic commitment to the collection demonstrates that he saw it not only as an important act of welfare and fellowship, but also as a significant visual teaching aid for a range of doctrines which included worship, discipleship, community and the gospel itself.

23

Enough Is Enough
2 Corinthians 8:6–15

> Because giving is related to the heart of the gospel, it should also be at the heart of the Christian life.

Paul has begun his appeal to the Corinthians to be generous in their giving by quoting the example of the Macedonian churches: "In the midst of a very severe trial, their overflowing joy and their extreme poverty welled up in rich generosity" (8:2). The next section begins with the connecting phrase "So we urged Titus . . ." (v. 6). In the light of the Macedonian response, Paul is encouraging the Corinthians to be ready to respond to the visit of Titus, and to complete their collection for the Judean churches. He introduces further incentives in order to encourage them to give, and these should shape our motivation too.

1. Generous Giving Should Be Part of a Rounded Christian Life (8:7–8)

We have already noted (8:1) that Paul uses the word "grace" frequently here, and he does so twice in verses 6 and 7. The grace of giving is just as significant in the Christian life as faith, or knowledge or love. Since the Corinthians excel in all of these gifts, Paul urges them to excel in the grace of giving too (v. 7). It is part of mature Christian discipleship, not an optional extra.

This requires a change of thinking for many Christians, for whom giving is quite marginal to their discipleship. This is often because we have made the mistake of compartmentalizing our lives, with some features of the Christian faith marked out as more spiritual than others. But the reality and quality of our worship are measured not solely by our verbal responses in prayer and song, but also when the collection plate is passed. The grace of giving should be as central a feature of our service as all other aspects of our spiritual life. It is part of God's call to a rounded Christian maturity. So Paul does not exercise his apostolic authority by issuing a command that the Corinthians should give to the collection (v. 8). Rather, he expects their giving to flow naturally as a result of their love and sincere commitment to Christ and to one another. They shouldn't need to be bullied into action, because the grace of giving is a willing and joyful expression of true spirituality.

2. Generous Giving Is a Response to the Grace of the Gospel (8:9)

Here Paul provides us with a theological gem: "For you know the grace of our Lord Jesus Christ, that though he was rich, yet for your sake he became poor, so that you through his poverty might become rich" (v. 9). In the span of a few words he expresses the profound mystery of Christ's incarnation, with its implications of sacrificial giving on the part of God's Son and undeserved riches for us.

It is quite common for Paul to support his ethical appeals with a theological argument, and here he introduces one of the finest expressions of the nature of the gospel as part of his encouragement to the Corinthians to be generous in supporting the needs of others. Look what Christ has done for you! Try to imagine the extent of his sacrifice in leaving the riches of heaven and entering our world in poverty. And reflect on the spiritual riches which are yours as a result of Christ's generosity.

A verse such as this places Christian giving in perspective. The one who calls us to give liberally is the one who was rich yet for our sakes became poor. God's grace has been shown in his generosity to those in desperate need, and now our giving should reflect something of that generosity. This is why the whole of Paul's argument in chapters 8 and 9 is based around the idea of grace. As Jesus himself expressed it, "Freely you have received; freely give" (Matt 10:8).

3. Generous Giving Is a Matter of Responsible Stewardship (8:10–12)

Here Paul begins by arguing for the importance of completion (2 Cor 8:10–12). The Corinthians had begun well. A year earlier they had been the first enthusiastic participants (v. 10), taking up the offering regularly. But now they need to complete the good work (v. 11). Paul implies that this is not only important for the recipients but is also "best for you" (v. 10). Bringing the project to completion is part of their responsible and joyful duty, and it will bring its own rewards. Once again, it is part of discipleship. Having put your hand to the plough, don't look back. Having started to build the tower, make sure you finish (see Luke 9:62; 14:23–30).

God's assessment of their giving would not be based on the quantity of cash in the box, but on the proportion of their giving in relation to their means (v. 12). Here Paul states the same principle as appears in the story of the widow's "mite," as it is sometimes called. The person who gives the most is not necessarily the most generous. Generosity has to do with the resources with which you have been entrusted, the proper stewardship of what God has given you. The widow's contribution of two very small copper coins was recorded in Scripture (Mark 12:41–44) because it represented a sacrificial gift in relation to her total resources. And in the same way, God does not expect us to give what we do not have (2 Cor 8:12). Rather, the grace of giving is a willing, joyful and sacrificial response to the gospel, in proportion to the financial resources for which we are responsible.

4. Generous Giving Leads to Equality (8:13–15)

The Corinthians should be contributing to the needs of others as part of Christian fellowship – not so that others will live in luxury while the Corinthians suffer hardship (8:13), but so that there will be a just distribution of resources (v. 14). Should the day come when the Corinthians face economic pressure, then the same generosity would be expected from the Christians in the north. It is part of reciprocal commitment and solidarity within Christian fellowship.

Some writers suggest that Paul is not necessarily limiting the subject to money: the Corinthians can make a financial contribution to the needs of the believers in Judea, and the Judean believers can continue to share the riches of the gospel with the Gentile believers to the south. Either way, the primary point of Paul's encouragement is that there is a fundamental incentive in Christian fellowship, and that is to ensure that the needs of each person are met. That in turn demands generosity on the part of those who have the resources to share.

Quoting from the story of the manna in the wilderness (Exod 16:18), Paul makes the point that such giving is not meant to create further inequalities but rather to ensure that everyone will have enough (2 Cor 8:15). This was part of the miracle of God's provision in Exodus 16: whether a person collected much or little, each had enough for their needs. So, Paul says, the grace of giving will provide appropriately for all.

In many countries around the world, including wealthy Western nations, the divisions between the rich and the poor are sharper than ever. None of us can avoid the challenges of these verses, with their strong incentives to be committed to the needs of others. Whether within our own Christian community, or in the context of the inequalities between nations, we need to reflect on how our giving is shaped by the themes Paul has identified: our discipleship, our commitment to the gospel, our stewardship of God's resources and our concern for justice and equality.

Questions

1. In encouraging the church to give, why is it important to present this ministry as reflecting the grace of the gospel?

2. How aware are you of the needs of others within your own Christian community, and within the church worldwide? How can you become more informed?

3. Paul does not mention "tithing" (see Lev 27:30–32; Deut 26:12). Why do you think this is? Can giving a tenth be a good rule for Christians to follow? (See box labelled "Tithing," p. 124.)

24

Take Care
2 Corinthians 8:16–9:5

We need to avoid any suspicion of dishonesty when handling money. Practical measures are needed to avoid potential criticism or temptation.

The seriousness with which Paul viewed the collection is expressed not only in his appeal to the Corinthians to complete the task and send in their generous contribution, but also by his responsible management of the entire operation. This section introduces a series of practical steps Paul took to ensure that all went well, and each says something about the significance of wise stewardship and giving in the context of Christian fellowship.

1. Faithful Servants (8:16–19)

First, Paul refers to several of his fellow workers who were partners with him in this ministry. Titus was a great supporter of the project (8:16–17). He was ready to travel to Corinth and was enthusiastic about receiving their money. He was accompanied by a well-known brother – so well known that Paul doesn't need to name him. Significantly, Paul identifies him in relation to his faithful service to the gospel (v. 18). He was the specially selected delegate of the churches to help with the collection programme (v. 19). And there was a further partner, referred to in verse 22, also marked out as "zealous," or eager.

Paul is demonstrating here that the collection of the offering was committed to faithful, reliable servants of the churches, who were committed to the gospel

117

and were very trustworthy. In Acts 6, when the church needed to appoint people to relieve the apostles of time-consuming practical tasks, they chose men "full of the Spirit" (Acts 6:3). The point is that whatever the task within the Christian community, spiritual qualifications are needed. This is important in the area of financial management, whether counting the Sunday offering or administering the funds of a Christian organization. Paul's fellow workers were some of the best, and he could rely on their faithful ministry and enthusiastic participation as people of integrity.

2. Careful Administration (8:20–21)

Such use of trusted fellow workers was part of a policy of wise management. Paul spent considerable effort in ensuring not only that things were done properly, but that they were *seen* to be done properly (8:21). First, fellow workers were essential if Paul was to avoid any potential criticism (v. 20). The offering was clearly a substantial sum, so Paul needed fellow travellers to ensure adequate protection. Working as a team is important in every aspect of church life because of the special benefits of shared gifts, mutual support and encouragement, but also accountability. This is particularly important in the area of financial administration. Second, as we have seen, such fellow workers need to be trusted colleagues with the right spiritual and practical qualities for the job.

It is important to be honest here. The temptation to misuse funds probably comes a close second to sexual temptation, not only among leaders but among all believers, although leaders sometimes face more opportunities to be tempted than the rest of us. Since it can be a device of Satan to exploit potential weaknesses, it is always important in church affairs to ensure that there is careful administration similar to that which Paul put in place here. Even the most trustworthy treasurer needs others to work with him in counting money, signing cheques or making bank transfers, so that we take "pains to do what is right, not only in the eyes of the Lord but also in the eyes of men" (v. 21).

3. Solidarity between the Churches (8:18–19, 23–24)

This section also reinforces the theme of the early part of the chapter: the offering itself is an expression of Christian fellowship (8:4). The way in which Paul administered the collection also reflected the corporate solidarity of the churches. He refers to this when commenting on his fellow workers: the brother who is "praised by all the churches" was "chosen by the churches to accompany us as we carry the offering" (vv. 18–19). Clearly there was a sense of ownership of the project, with the churches involved in selecting the team of helpers. Similarly, he reinforces the sense of partnership when he refers to Titus as a "co-worker among you," and the brothers as "representatives of the churches" (v. 23). This is not just the initiative of Paul or of Titus. This is a shared project of the churches, all of whom feel a sense of engagement in making it happen.

This is also part of Paul's appeal to the Corinthians. If his fellow workers are representatives of the churches, then it is important that the Corinthians respect them, welcoming them as they arrive to take up the offering, and demonstrating their love for their fellow believers "so that the churches can see it" (v. 24). Show others why I am so confident in you, Paul says; don't let me down, after all I have said about you, but prove your love by the grace of giving. This practical commitment to give was part of their solidarity with others.

Many of us know the special bonds of fellowship with other believers that arise from the practical fellowship of financial support. Whether we are giving or receiving, when there is grace in the process there is also a deepening of fellowship. Being part of a Christian community demands generosity, and generosity in turn strengthens the sense of Christian community.

4. Honouring the Lord (8:19, 21–22)

To reinforce the fact that the offering is part of their service to Christ, Paul refers several times to the importance of honouring the Lord. The administration of the offering by the team of fellow workers was "to honour the Lord himself" (8:19). The careful procedures they adopted were to ensure that everything was done correctly "in the eyes of the Lord" (v. 21). And the faithful partners in taking up the offering were "an honour to Christ" (v. 23).

Nothing was done in a haphazard or casual way; no opportunity was given for criticism; nothing was allowed to dishonour the name of Christ. This should be true of every aspect of our work in the church. Our purpose is not to build our own organization or reputation, or to attract attention to our own skills and successes, but to honour Christ. That's why the church is here.

5. Ready for Action (9:1–5)

Just as Paul used the example of the Macedonians to encourage the Corinthians to give generously, so he had apparently boasted of the Corinthians in order to encourage others to give too (9:2). It was a successful strategy, since the Corinthian enthusiasm "stirred most of them to action" (v. 2). And he explains this to the believers in Corinth in order to urge them to live up to his boasting (v. 3). Paul wants to ensure that the Corinthians are not embarrassed. It would be a pity if the Macedonian believers had turned up in Corinth with high expectations of Corinthian generosity, only to find that the church was grudging in its attitude and mean with its resources (v. 4).

Once again employing the wise pastoral practice of affirmation, Paul is sure they are keen to help, that their generous offering is certain and he does not need to stress the point. Instead, he is giving them notice that his partners will be arriving to tidy up the final arrangements and to collect their freewill offering (v. 5).

As Paul has written in chapter 8, it is simply a matter of keeping their promise, completing the task and giving joyfully. He repeats on several occasions that their gift should not be grudging, but a response of free generosity (8:4, 10, 11, 12; 9:5, 7). In the light of the incentives that Paul is presenting, there should be no doubt about our response. But before the chapter closes, Paul has a further significant principle to teach us that will motivate us still further.

Questions

1. What are the essential safeguards which will ensure good financial administration in today's church?

2. Are there opportunities for strengthening your solidarity with other churches in co-operative financial projects?

3. Paul is stressing that genuine giving should be a freewill offering (9:5). What are the main motivations in your giving?

25

Harvest Thanksgiving
2 Corinthians 9:6–15

> **Giving creates a ripple effect for the benefit of all concerned, bringing praise to God.**

In the final section of this appeal for generous giving, Paul introduces a basic principle which is true in nature and true in grace: you reap what you sow. "Remember this: whoever sows sparingly will also reap sparingly, and whoever sows generously will also reap generously" (9:6). He spells out the implications of this simple proverb in the verses which follow, demonstrating that the act of giving starts an important chain reaction.

1. Sowing and Reaping (9:6–12)

Just as a farmer determines how much seed to use and how many fields to prepare, so each of us must determine in our hearts what we are to give (9:7). This is a voluntary decision, and it will in due course result in a harvest. Paul's use of the agricultural picture is not unusual. Several proverbs use the image (Prov 11:24–25; 19:17; 22:8–9), and Jesus himself taught that there was a relationship between giving and receiving when he explained: "For with the measure you use, it will be measured to you" (Luke 6:38).

Paul's purpose is not to provoke a selfish response – "the more I give, the more I can get back." Sometimes the fundraising techniques of certain Christian organizations appeal to such motives. Michael Thompson tells the story of one radio evangelist who promised: "Send us $20 and God will give

121

you back three times what you give us." He received a letter from a listener with the sensible suggestion: "Why don't you give us the $20, and you'll receive what you need three times over!"[1]

The point of this section of Paul's letter is to enlarge our vision of the dynamics of giving – the ripple effects of our generosity in all kinds of directions. There will be an impressive harvest from our investment, which Paul will explain in these verses. So each of us should give willingly (v. 7) and cheerfully. (It is often pointed out that this verse could literally be translated "God loves a hilarious giver," expressing the sense of abandon and enthusiasm which the Macedonians clearly exhibited.)

Paul begins by focusing on God as the source of all blessings. He is the one who provides all we need. In just one verse (v. 8), Paul refers to "all" or "every" four times in order to demonstrate God's ability to care for us and to enable us to be providers in return. Significantly, grace is at the centre once again. Whatever the circumstances of our lives, God will meet our needs.

To buttress his argument, Paul quotes from Psalm 112 to show, not only that God is constantly generous in his provision to the needy, but also that his generosity in turn will result in the righteous act of sharing our resources with others in need. Just as God provides the seed for the sower and oversees the process of growth, he will also be at work in our lives, encouraging more acts of righteousness that will in turn produce an even greater harvest.

He then explains the three ways in which there will be a productive result: First, the giver will be enriched (9:11). Paul explains that the Corinthians will be "enriched in every way." God's provision for them will mean that they will be able to be still more generous, for that is the way God works. He provides more so we can give more. Part of the enrichment will be the fact that others will be praying for the givers (v. 14), which is part of the response of fellowship which giving will generate.

Second, their giving supplies the needs of God's people (v. 12). The "service" of giving is an act of worship (the word Paul uses is the word for "liturgy"), and clearly the initial reason for the collection was to meet the needs of hard-pressed Christians in Jerusalem.

There is a third consequence which is the most significant of all. Paul refers to it repeatedly, and that is that God will be praised. Their "generosity will result in thanksgiving to God" (v. 11), is "also overflowing in many expressions

---

1. Michael Thompson, *Transforming Grace: A Study of 2 Corinthians* (Oxford: The Bible Reading Fellowship, 1998), 84.

of thanks to God" (v. 12), and will provoke people to "praise God" (v. 13; see also 1:11; 4:15).

As we have seen, when Christians give sacrificially and generously, it reflects the fact that they have experienced the grace of the gospel and understood the dynamics of Christian fellowship. Both of these points are referred to in this section. In verse 13 Paul explains that the convincing proof of their acceptance of the gospel was the obedience which accompanied it – in other words, their practical commitment to giving. And then in the same verse he refers to their "generosity in sharing with them and with everyone else." Giving has to do with our commitment to the gospel of God and the people of God. When generosity is seen it should therefore generate a response of thanksgiving and worship to God. Paul also hints at the ripple effect through his use of language: their giving "overflows" in many expressions of thanks to God (v. 12).

2. The Harvest Thanksgiving (9:13–15)

As the chapter draws to a close, Paul has still more to say about God's grace. For when the Corinthians give, other believers will know that this is the result of the "surpassing grace" God had given them (9:14). It is this thought which leads Paul to his concluding doxology. If giving produces such a wonderful harvest, it all flows from the initial act of God's generosity towards us in the "indescribable gift" of his Son (v. 15). The word for "thanks" in verse 15 is actually the Greek word *charis*, which usually means "grace." Everything about these two chapters breathes that spirit. God has been overwhelmingly generous to us, who least deserved his gracious provision. Now, as an expression of our worship and thanksgiving, we are called to reflect that grace in the way in which we give to others. His final expression of praise reminds us that in the coming of Christ, in his living and dying, there can be no higher standard for our giving and no greater motivation.

"Thanks be to God for his indescribable gift!" (v. 15).

Questions

1. If there is a formal collection taken during your church services, how can this "offering" become more truly a part of your worship?

2. Can you think of ways in which you have witnessed the "ripple effect" of Christian giving?

3. How does your group understand the idea of "fellowship"? Make a list together of the essential ingredients of fellowship.

Tithing

The word "tithing" comes from the payment of a tenth. In the Old Testament tithing was an important community principle, for it not only represented an expression of gratitude to God but was also the means whereby provision was made for the poor, for the Levites and for the priests. It was not only money that was given, but also crops, fruits and animals.

In 2 Corinthians 8, Paul demonstrates that, like Jesus, he does not confine giving to a tenth, but instead highlights the themes of generosity and sacrifice. Paul isn't keen on strict rules; he is much more enthusiastic about overflowing gratitude.

So, should Christians tithe today? It certainly would be a great place to start! But in some senses the debate about careful tithing could become rather sterile. These two chapters in 2 Corinthians encourage us to give with joyful and sacrificial generosity. There is certainly a case for planned giving (1 Cor 16:1–2), but Paul's appeal is clearly linked to the grace of the gospel. In other words, God didn't limit his giving by careful calculation. Jesus's total self-giving provides the benchmark for our attitude and motivation (Matt 10:8).

A practical solution has been proposed with the idea of a "graduated tithe." This proposes that we should decide on a standard of living and then give 10 percent of that amount. Then, say, for every $100 we receive above that standard, we should increase our giving still further (perhaps a further 5 percent), until we eventually reach the position where we are giving away 100 percent of all additional income. Such figures will vary according to our culture and our circumstances, but some form of practical encouragement towards generosity is worth devising. What comes across from Paul's encouragements in 2 Corinthians is this: our giving should express the grace of the gospel.

Section 4

Paul Exerts His Authority

2 Corinthians 10:1–13:14

26

True Authority
2 Corinthians 10:1–11

> **Godly leadership does not borrow from secular ideas but is modelled on Christ.**

The change of tone in the final four chapters of the letter is so marked that commentators have varying views about how the letter was constructed. Are these final chapters a separate letter – perhaps the "painful letter" to which Paul had referred in 2:3–4? Or did Paul receive news from Corinth which affected him so deeply that it provoked a much more assertive style of writing, warning the Corinthians about the dangers of the false apostles whose influence seemed to be ever more pervasive? Some of these ideas are mentioned at the end of this section, but whatever the reason, there is a marked change of mood and writing style as we enter the final chapters.

For one thing, Paul uses irony – even a degree of sarcasm – as he responds to the accusations made against him. The false teachers in Corinth had certain expectations of a spiritual leader, expectations that were shaped by the Greek culture of the day. Leaders were eloquent orators, with an impressive physical presence; "weakness" was not a word in their vocabulary. As spiritual gurus, there was also something "other-worldly" about them; they would claim to have mystical experiences, special revelations, a spiritual hotline which marked them out as special.

Paul responds with a series of passionate arguments, each of which tells us something not only about Paul's calling as an apostle but also about the features we should look for in all true Christian leadership. Paul is not protecting his touchy honour nor is he concerned to defend his own reputation at all costs, but he is motivated by entirely different concerns. He is deeply concerned for the welfare of the Corinthian believers and wants to be sure that they are not captured by false notions of the gospel. His fierce response is motivated not by personal annoyance but by compassion for others and a conviction that he must defend the gospel itself.

1. His Model Is Christ (10:1–2)

Paul faced a dilemma as he confronted the charges of the false teachers. On the one hand, they implied that he was nothing other than a big talker. There was nothing impressive about him, and although he tried to exercise authority in his letters, in reality he was a weakling. His bark was worse than his bite. He was timid when he came face to face with them (10:1). So doing nothing in the face of such accusations would only confirm the Corinthians in their suspicions: he was no apostle, he was a weak-kneed fake. On the other hand, to reply to such criticism with an aggressive letter would do the same: "There he goes again," the Corinthians would say, "writing with such 'boldness' but from the safe distance of a few hundred miles."

The opening words of the chapter, therefore, are especially significant. Paul's model for his leadership is Christ himself. His appeal to the Corinthians is on the basis of "the humility and gentleness of Christ" (v. 1). The qualities with which Paul wishes to be identified are not the brash and loud-mouthed qualities of a showman, or the manipulative oratorical skills of a politician, or the heroic achievements of a Greek god. He wants to be identified with Jesus – with the controlled strength of the incarnate Lord. But meekness and gentleness should not be taken to mean passivity. When occasion demanded, Jesus was ready for straight talking and tough action. And so was Paul. He appeals to the Corinthians to set their house in order so that, when he next visits, he will not have to exercise as much discipline as he presently anticipates (v. 2). He will take bold action if this is needed (v. 6), but his style is not like that of the false teachers. He is not a spiritual superstar living in some kind of mystical space somewhere above the planet. He is part of the rough and tumble of this world (v. 3), just as Jesus was. But neither are his methods secular; his weapons are not the weapons of this world. How does he wage war against false teachers?

2. His Weapon Is Truth (10:3–6)

In several of his letters Paul mentions that Christians are equipped for spiritual warfare with the weapons which God supplies (2 Cor 6:6–7; Eph 6:14–17;

1 Thess 5:8). They include the truth of the gospel, the word of God, prayer and faith, all empowered by the Holy Spirit. Here Paul describes such weapons as powerful and effective (2 Cor 10:4).

Paul is especially concerned about the ideological battle, the battle for hearts and minds. He wants to show the false teachers that the wisdom of this world is foolishness, and that true apostleship is founded not on human wisdom or intellectual pretension, but on the gospel of Christ. He says much the same in 1 Corinthians: "Where is the wise person? Where is the teacher of the law? Where is the philosopher of this age? Has not God made foolish the wisdom of the world? . . . God was pleased through the foolishness of what was preached to save those who believe" (1 Cor 1:20–22).

The message of the gospel is able to demolish those strongholds that resist Christ's rule (2 Cor 10:5). Paul's purpose is to take captive every thought for obedience to Christ (v. 5). The false teachers in Corinth need to submit in obedience to Christ (v. 6). But there is also a wider application. True spiritual warfare is to enter enemy territory and, by the power of the gospel and the Spirit, confront every obstacle that will prevent total allegiance to Jesus Christ.

He expresses his concern that, should the false teachers fail to obey the true gospel, disciplinary action will be needed. He wants to be sure that the church is behind him ("once your obedience is complete," v. 6), but he will not withhold punishment if it is warranted. He goes on to explain the foundation for his authority.

3. His Authority Is God-Given (10:7–8)

Paul next outlines the foundation for his apostleship. He is not afraid of his apostleship being tested, but he wants the test to be fair.

First, like all true believers, he belongs to Christ (10:7). If some in Corinth were parading their spiritual credentials, they should remember that Paul has met the risen Christ, and that he has been called and commissioned by him, as he has explained so fully in earlier parts of the letter. He is their spiritual father, as he will stress in the next chapter, and therefore has God-given authority among them.

Next, he explains that his intentions are to build them up (10:8; 13:10); even what appear to be harsh words are motivated by a desire to be constructive. He is not ashamed or apologetic about that calling from the Lord (10:8). But neither does he want to be misunderstood. The apparently harsh rebukes which he has to issue are not to frighten them but to strengthen them. The fatherly discipline which he has to introduce is a necessary corrective if they are to be true to the gospel.

4. His Life Is Consistent (10:9–11)

Finally, as befits an apostle of Christ, he acts with complete integrity. Although he is accused of being one thing on paper and another in person (10:10), he insists that he is completely consistent. What he says, he will do (v. 11). He will discipline those who need it and punish disobedience if that is required (v. 6). In the next chapter he will respond more directly to the suggestion of verse 10 that "he is unimpressive and his speaking amounts to nothing." These accusations were part of the whispering campaign against Paul that was clearly gathering momentum in Corinth. The Christians were in danger of believing the fake news of the "super-apostles" (11:5), whose view of Christian leadership owed more to secular models than to Christ.

This is one of the reasons this section of the letter is especially valuable to us. For in our world, Christian leaders can be tempted to build their reputation and shape their style on the shallow fashions (10:4) of today's culture. Instead of the meekness and gentleness of Christ, they become dictators – "little tin gods," as J. B. Phillips once expressed it.[1] Instead of using the weapons of gospel truth, they rely on the force of personality, the dazzle of the performer or the manipulative oratory of a salesperson. Instead of the authority of Christ and his word, they become authoritarian, lacking the humility of a servant of Christ. And their lives lack the fundamental integrity of deeds matching words.

This section represents Paul's opening volley in a sustained attack on the false apostles, but he has revealed the qualities which all true servants of the Lord should imitate.

Questions

1. What does the word "meekness" mean to many people today? (Some translations use the word "meekness" instead of "humility" in 10:1.) In what sense was Christ meek, and how should we follow his example?

2. What can we learn from Paul's example about how to manage a controversy in the church?

3. What does it mean to take our thoughts captive in obedience to Christ (10:5)?

---

1. 1 Peter 5:3 in J. B. Phillips New Testament.

The Unity of 2 Corinthians

The sudden shift of gear when we arrive at chapter 10 of 2 Corinthians is one of several examples of marked change which has led to a great deal of discussion about the unity of the letter. Instead of being one coherent essay, it seems like a "cut and paste" exercise. There is no doubt that Paul wrote each part, and that the Corinthians were the recipients. But it almost seems as though different messages have been pulled together to make the one letter.

There is, for example, the long detour of 2:14–7:1. Within that there is the small section of 6:14–7:1 which some feel doesn't quite fit. Then there are the two chapters about the collection (8 and 9) which seem to appear from nowhere and disappear just as suddenly. But the main debate has focused around the final four chapters of the letter, because of the very different tone and style of writing which we find there. Whereas Paul was rejoicing at a new harmony with the Corinthians and their "godly sorrow" (7:6–11), now it seems that they are still suspicious of him (e.g. 11:7–11) and guilty of unrepentance (12:21).

There are three broad views about this section of the letter. First, some suggest that it could be the so-called "severe" (or tearful) letter to which Paul referred earlier (2:3; 7:12). It is a section which reads like an extended rebuke, and so perhaps it was the earlier tearful letter pasted on to complete our 2 Corinthians at a much later date. The main problem with this view is that there is no evidence in the Greek manuscripts to support the idea. There is no reason to suppose that the letter ended with chapter 9; and there is no evidence of the usual opening greetings that might accompany chapter 10 if it were the beginning of the severe letter.

Second, many people argue that it is one letter, and that there are enough recurring themes to demonstrate its unity. In many of his letters Paul moves from encouragement to rebuke, and we should not be surprised that there are signs of agitation and discontinuity. Paul was hardly relaxed when he wrote the letter, and the range of emotions which he displays are consistent with the controversies he was addressing and the many pressures he was feeling. But here again the case is not clear. In particular, the change in the final four chapters is so substantial and unexpected that we cannot explain it away too easily.

This has led to a third view, which perhaps has the greatest merit. Paul wrote chapters 1 to 9, but then received some further bad news about the state of the church. He decided to send both a rebuke and an encouragement to the believers, and it is this section, written some while after he had dictated chapters 1 to 9 and after receiving further news, that makes up chapters 10 to 13.

It seems fair to conclude that 2 Corinthians is therefore one letter, even if its writing was interrupted. Throughout the letter we find a mixture of affirmation and rebuke, and many indications of Paul's concern and love for the Corinthians. Most significantly of all, we find the theme of strength through weakness (12:10) holding the letter together.

27

The Real Reward

2 Corinthians 10:12–18

> **It is easy to fall into the trap of self-commendation, but it is God's approval that matters.**

As we read Paul's defence, we sense something of the discomfort he obviously feels. This is not simply the pain of being criticized, but the discomfort of having to write about himself, of "boasting about" or "commending" himself. But the Corinthians have forced him into it, and for the rest of the letter he will have to "boast" in order to expose the empty rhetoric of the teachers who are capturing the minds and hearts of the believers for whom he cares so much. It goes against the grain, as we shall see, but Paul skilfully turns the tables on those for whom such boasting is an integral part of their self-centred lives.

1. The Folly of Self-Commendation (10:12)

Paul mocks his critics in Corinth by showing how foolish they are to commend themselves (10:12). They doubtless arrived in Corinth carrying special letters of commendation – written and signed by themselves – so it's no surprise when in fact they meet their own standards! As Paul will show in this next section, the real test of authenticity in Christian ministry is not what kind of testimonial you can write for yourself, but the abiding fruit of your work demonstrated by lives changed, churches established and Christians making headway in the faith. Paul argues the case by explaining the foundation for his "boasting."

2. The Basis of Paul's Calling (10:13–14)

First, Paul demonstrates once again that he is a man of integrity: he will not boast of work which he did not achieve. Rather, the evidence of his apostleship is seen in the "sphere of service" God gave him (10:13). Paul is describing the territory which was his special responsibility. This was the result of the division of labour agreed upon in Galatians 2, and it included Corinth.

Although it was a negotiated agreement among the apostles, notice how he sees this territory as his God-given responsibility (v. 13). This was why he poured his energies into his apostolic labours, why he invested so much in seeking to establish the church in Corinth, and why he now felt so distraught at the thought of the church rejecting not only its apostle but potentially the gospel itself. The evidence of his apostleship was the fact that he had brought the gospel to them. If he had not arrived at Corinth, then of course there would be no foundation for his boasting (v. 14). But the believers in Corinth knew how he had laboured among them; their very existence as a church was due to his efforts. Paul was not seeking credit for himself from the work of others (vv. 15–16) but was proving his God-given calling by the results which would have been clear to the Corinthian believers themselves. "You yourselves are our letter [of recommendation]," as he said earlier in the letter (3:2).

3. The Focus of Apostolic Ministry (10:15–16)

Indeed, his hope was that his ministry could continue in Corinth, and he refers to two significant potential developments (10:15–16). First, *depth*. The work having begun, it was vital that it continued. He wanted to see their faith continue to grow. This was central to Paul's missionary strategy, as he explains to other churches (Col 1:28–29; 2:6–7). He was concerned with depth as well as breadth; he wanted to see mature congregations made up of godly disciples, not just statistics of the number of converts in each city.

But second, *mission*. He always had an eye on the next evangelistic challenge (2 Cor 10:16). Alongside his concern to consolidate the work he retained his pioneering vision. He was hoping that a strong sense of fellowship with the Corinthians would provide the platform from which to launch further missionary initiatives, "so that we can preach the gospel in the regions beyond you" (v. 16).

The twin themes expressed in these verses are significant for churches and missionaries of every generation. The history of the church is littered with examples of projects that have begun well but have not been finished. We are quite good at starting things, not so good at seeing them through. But Paul was always concerned to see faith continue to grow (verse 15). And alongside the demands of nurturing, teaching, pastoring and strengthening a church, we need to keep alert to the regions beyond (v. 16), where the gospel has yet to be proclaimed. This might be a commitment to our immediate neighbourhood, or a commitment to the missionary challenge in another part of the world – ideally, both!

4. The Reward that Matters (10:17–18)

In contrast to the self-centred claims of Paul's critics in Corinth, with their inflated egos, neatly presented testimonials and persistent self-commendation, Paul quotes from Jeremiah to press home his point. If you are going to boast about anything, don't focus on your own achievements. Don't glory in your work for the Lord, but glory in the Lord of the work (10:17). For what really matters in Christian service is the Lord's approval (v. 18).

The closing verse of the chapter is therefore a great corrective and a great encouragement. Some of us might be tempted to be proud of our achievements as Christians, or we might see our gifts or status within the Christian community as providing important personal fulfilment and evidence of our value as church members. Some of our churches or organizations might be tempted to publish success stories of great achievements, glad to be known as centres of Christian excellence and secretly proud of our effective ministry. For all of us tempted to think in this way, Paul reminds us: "it is not the one who commends himself who is approved" (v. 18).

There are many churches which don't make the Christian newspapers, and have no glossy websites, but which are consistently faithful in working for the Lord in a tough environment with little obvious reward. In all churches there are Christians who are quietly serving Christ, often working very sacrificially and usually without recognition, acknowledgment or thanks. Is it really worthwhile? To such Christians, Paul's words should be a deep encouragement: the real reward is the Lord's commendation.

Questions

1. What would you say are the qualities of a successful Christian leader?

2. In what ways can our churches be guilty of self-commendation?

3. How can we avoid measuring ourselves by one another (10:12)? Is it wrong to have role models? Is there a right and a wrong way to compare ourselves with others? What are they?

4. What kind of concern does your church have for "regions beyond" (10:16), whether local or international, and in what ways can that be encouraged?

28

True or False

2 Corinthians 11:1–15

> **The gospel message is always in danger of being distorted, not least by false teachers whose deceptive message can be a severe threat. Every church must keep alert to the danger.**

The next section of Paul's letter has a deepening intensity both in terms of his strident criticism of the false apostles and his passionate concern for the well-being of the Corinthians. It is powerful stuff. His writing displays raw emotion. And no wonder, for the newcomers in Corinth were evidently seducing the Corinthian Christians from their love for Christ and their commitment to the gospel.

Paul is outraged at such deceptive behaviour and wastes no time in exposing these self-styled "super-apostles" for what they are – false apostles, deceitful workmen, servants of Satan himself (11:13–15). It's tough writing, but it is important that we take note of what Paul has to say, because every church will encounter subtle internal attacks, the devil masquerading as an angel. It is wise to be alert to his schemes. In verses 1–6 Paul describes what has happened to the Corinthians.

1. A Subtle Distraction (11:1–3)

Paul's irony continues as he tries to wake up the Corinthians to what is happening. He hopes they will put up with a little more of his "foolishness"

(11:1), which is one of the charges against him. They're doing well listening to his crazy ranting and raving, so perhaps they can take a little more, he says.

His passion is expressed first in his description of his jealous love for them. As he wrote in the last chapter, they are the result of his labour, the fruit of his costly missionary endeavours. He is a spiritual father whose loving duty was to see his daughter presented as a pure virgin to her husband (v. 2). So his present concern, the sense of horror he expresses at what is happening in Corinth, is motivated by his "godly jealousy" for them.

Can't they see what is happening? Flirting with a stranger will eventually lead them to desert their husband. And this deception will have catastrophic consequences. The seriousness of the situation is demonstrated by Paul's comparison: it is like Eve being deceived by the serpent's cunning (v. 3). It is subtle, it is Satanic and ultimately it leads to destruction. If they continue to listen to the false apostles, their minds will be captured, and they will be led away from devotion to Christ.

2. A Different Jesus (11:4–6)

In his letter to the Galatians Paul also warns the believers that there are some who preach "another gospel" (Gal 1:6). In verse 4 of this chapter, Paul uses very similar language – a different Jesus, a different spirit, a different gospel. The Corinthians were swallowing the teaching of the newcomers, without realizing that it was a betrayal of the true gospel. As we have seen, there is some debate about the identity of these false apostles, but it is generally agreed that they were Judaizers: Christians from a Jewish background who were insisting that when Gentiles became Christians they should observe some of the laws of Moses (see box labelled "Paul's Opponents," p. 43).

We have also seen how they were influenced by the culture around them, with their fundamental ideas concerning Christian ministry and leadership deeply influenced by secular rather than gospel values. In other words, they were true believers, part of God's family, but their approach to Christian living was fundamentally skewed and distorted.

It is this which made their influence all the more dangerous. They were not enemies from outside, but believers from within the family. They were not teaching obvious heresy, but a subtle distortion of orthodox truth. They pretended to be "super-apostles," with their persuasive eloquence, but they were not apostles of the true gospel – the gospel which has the weakness of the crucified Jesus at its heart. It was "a different gospel from the one you accepted," Paul says (2 Cor 11:4), but the tragedy was the ease with which the Corinthians accepted it. Paul's defence is that, although he might not be as eloquent as his opponents, true apostleship is not dependent on eloquence (vv. 5–6). He has the knowledge of the gospel, and he explained that consistently – "in every way" – when he was with them.

It is not easy for Christians today to spot the subtle distractions which will take us away from a sincere devotion to Christ, but we should learn from these verses that vigilance is essential. When someone preaches a Jesus who promises an easy discipleship, or presents a gospel which removes weakness and promises that we will ride high on a success-orientated spirituality, it is time to become suspicious. For it is likely that this is a different Jesus and a different gospel from that which the New Testament presents to us. It might look good, and feel good, but it will lead our minds away from sincere devotion to Christ.

3. Genuine Service (11:7–12)

A further accusation made by Paul's critics was that his lifestyle showed that he was not a true spiritual leader. He could hardly be called an apostle if he engaged in such menial tasks as making tents! Again, the value system of those who criticized Paul was shaped more by the Greek culture of the day than by the gospel. For the Greeks, a leader and orator presented a substantial lecture fee to his audiences. And the Greeks viewed manual labour as the lowest form of activity, certainly not an appropriate task for a true apostle.

First, Paul says, he was able to bring the gospel to them without charge, in humble service, because other Christians were supporting him (11:7–8). It was important that the Corinthians realized that, far from being a sin, this was motivated by a genuine desire to serve them and was supported by the generosity of fellow believers in Macedonia. Not only that, he genuinely wished to avoid being a burden to them (v. 9), and, whether through the support of other believers, or through his own tent-making, he would continue to adopt that attitude.

He is in the business of Christian service not for personal gain but for their well-being. And he asserts once again, in a forceful phrase, that he is acting with absolute integrity in these matters: "As surely as the truth of Christ is in me" (v. 10). He will not tolerate people implying that his ministry is for his personal benefit. Quite the opposite. He is happy to continue to boast that he has acted as he has entirely because he loves the Corinthians. And in another forceful phrase he insists that this is the case: "God knows I do!" (v. 11).

In fact, living in this way (avoiding unnecessary dependence on the Corinthians whom he served, and avoiding the charge of personal financial gain) was the way in which he could continue to undermine his critics (v. 12).

4. Deceitful Workmen (11:13–15)

Next Paul turns the tables. From defending his own behaviour, he moves to a direct attack on his critics. And he pulls no punches. He uses dramatic language – deceitful workmen, wolves in sheep's clothing, Satanic intruders (11:13–15). The point of his illustrations is to highlight their deception. They pretend to be spiritual leaders and apostles of Christ, but they are nothing of the sort. They only "masquerade as servants of righteousness" (v. 15). In reality, when the mask is stripped away, they are seen for what they are: servants of Satan himself. Their work, like their master's, is to deceive; and their destiny will be the same as his (v. 15).

At first sight this all seems to be rather intolerant. Surely Paul could express himself more graciously? They can't be all that bad! But for Paul to have gone soft at this point would have been a serious error. Few of us are ready for this kind of confrontation. But there may well be times within today's church when the veneer must be stripped away, and the evil influences of Satan have to be exposed. Certainly, this demands prayerful discernment, careful theological evaluation and the wisdom of the group. But there is a time for intolerance of error and for a defence of the truth as it is in Jesus.

Questions

1. What is it about our society today that makes it difficult for us to be intolerant with error? In what ways are our churches affected by such an emphasis on tolerance?

2. Are you aware of ways in which people, even within the Christian church, present a "different Jesus" or a "different gospel"? How can we keep alert to subtle distortions like this?

3. If we have seen people become Christians through our witness or the work of the church, do we feel a "godly jealousy" for their commitment to Christ, as Paul did for the Corinthians? What would this look like, and why does it matter?

29

Something to Be Proud Of
2 Corinthians 11:16–33

> In an extraordinary catalogue of "achievements,"
> Paul provides a list of credentials which makes
> weakness the main characteristic of his apostleship.

Paul's reluctance to continue his "boasting" comes out once again as he pursues the defence of his apostleship and the exposure of the false teachers. He does so to encourage the Corinthians to confront the distortions of the gospel which they appear to be accepting so readily. Such "self-confident boasting" (11:17) runs against the grain for Paul, but if they take him for a fool then he will play along. And he will adopt the same style as his opponents for the purpose of exposing them for what they are (v. 18). With his now familiar irony, he suggests that the Corinthians are making the mistake, in their supposed wisdom, of putting up with fools (the false teachers), so maybe they can cope with Paul too (v. 19)!

Using his characteristic sharp language, he speaks directly to the Corinthians about their own naivety in welcoming the false teachers. For they are not true apostles, with a compassionate concern for their well-being, but fakes, set on manipulating, exploiting and even abusing them (v. 20).

1. A Catalogue of Suffering (11:16–28)

Paul then starts a lengthy self-defence. He is still uncomfortable about having to tell his story in this way (11:21, 23), but after an explanation of his pedigree (a true Hebrew, a true descendant of Abraham, a true servant of Christ), he then provides a list of credentials which is the absolute opposite of what his opponents might expect. Instead of recording his great victories, it is a catalogue of his sufferings. Instead of proclaiming his great strengths, it exposes his weaknesses. And this is Paul's deliberate strategy, as he is to declare openly both here (v. 30) and in the next chapter (12:9).

Paul's list of weaknesses hardly needs comment. Reading it through as it stands has its own impact, amazing the reader as we see the range and intensity of the suffering he endured as an apostle. First, he lists the many occasions when he encountered opposition as he preached the gospel, from imprisonment to flogging. Frequently these experiences brought him close to death. Then he tells of the various physical dangers which accompanied his many miles of travelling and lists the dangers from bandits and false brothers. Alongside such perils, he says, he has suffered the physical and emotional drain of constant hard work, sleep deprivation, and the ill-effects of hunger and cold.

And in what appears as a short and insignificant postscript, he adds, "Besides everything else, I face daily the pressure of my concern for all the churches" (11:28). We know a little of that pressure from the Corinthian correspondence. But multiply this several times over, as we must for an apostle who founded so many congregations and whose pastoral heart was so large, and we have a further glimpse of the weight of responsibility and sense of pressure which Paul constantly endured.

2. What Makes an Apostle (11:29–31)

It is a very compact list, but it doesn't take too much imagination to reconstruct the sort of lifestyle which this man faced. Unlike these dazzling Corinthian "super-apostles," Paul recounts no stories of his victories, tells no stories of admiring crowds, lists no prestigious lectureships. He deliberately chooses to major on his weaknesses. Indeed, he seems to stress that weakness is his hallmark as an apostle (11:29).

Even the pull of sin, common to all Christians, is something with which this spiritual apostle identifies within himself (though another way of understanding verse 29 is to do with his sense of pastoral identification with the weak, and his sense of indignation about those who have been led into sin).

There is nothing super spiritual about Paul. He is no bionic superman, no spiritual guru, no hero in the classic traditions of the day. He is tired and bruised, frail and weak, an itinerant preacher of a foolish message.

He presses home the point in verse 30. If he is forced to boast of his achievements, and sing his praise in the manner of the false teachers, then he will sing from a different song-sheet than theirs: "I will boast of the things that show my weakness." Just as he did in verse 11 ('God knows I do!'), he can once again appeal to God as his witness (v. 31).

3. Being Let Down (11:32–33)

His final illustration adds a further touch of irony. In his list of "achievements," he adds the example of his hurried and embarrassing departure from Damascus (see Acts 9:23–25). The city was being guarded in the hope of capturing Paul, but he was dropped over the wall in a basket, and once he hit the ground, he ran away from Damascus as fast as he could. The great hero Paul! Would you have boasted about that kind of humiliating exit? It certainly didn't match the Corinthians' expectations of the leaders of the day. But Paul must have had a twinkle in his eye as he told the story and rounded off his CV. How about that one for an example of foolishness! It was just another instance of God's power being demonstrated in Paul's weakness.

In the next chapter his boasting will continue one stage further in order to highlight the paradox of the whole letter – the paradox of the gospel and of Christian ministry. But we should pause, before moving on, to draw some conclusions about Paul's catalogue.

Most obviously, *Paul is not afraid to declare his weaknesses*. We have already seen that Paul had learned the important lesson that such weaknesses are necessary in the Christian life. They teach us to be dependent on God, not on our own resources (2 Cor 1:9), and they therefore become the occasion for the display of God's grace and power (4:7; 12:9–10).

We can learn from this in our own culture which, like first-century Greek culture, mocks the fool and despises the weak. The Christian sub-culture might also be tempted to honour those who are persuasive and articulate, such as the successful church leaders who dress smartly and run state-of-the-art churches. Certainly there is a place for quality, and a necessary commitment to careful presentation for today's image-conscious generation. But sometimes our Christianity can seem squeaky-clean and manicured compared with the rough edges and frailties that were so obvious in Paul.

Second, *Paul is faithfully following his Master*. To be a servant of Christ, and to preach his gospel, will inevitably mean that our lives will be characterized by the same pattern as his. It will not be a life of comfort, for he had nowhere to lay his head; it will not be a life of acceptance, for his own people rejected him; it will not be a life immune from pain and suffering, for he walked the road to Gethsemane and Golgotha. But paradoxically, as Paul is demonstrating throughout this moving letter, it is ultimately a life which displays God's grace and power.

Questions

1. Would Paul's description of the characteristics of a leader shock your church as much as it would the believers in first-century Corinth?

2. "Surely the pastor shouldn't show his weaknesses. He's someone we look up to." Would you agree?

3. Are we tempted to think that some aspects of work in the church or in Christian service generally seem beneath our dignity? What does this say about our understanding of Christ's mission?

30

The Vision and the Thorn
2 Corinthians 12:1–10

The heart of Paul's testimony is that weakness is where we can specially experience God's grace and power.

Paul now moves to another sphere of his life about which, reluctantly, he feels compelled to speak. A further element in the Corinthians' expectation of a truly spiritual leader related to profound, mystical, other-worldly experiences. The false teachers fostered the delusion that, in line with the culture of the day, the leaders worthy of respect were those who seemed to walk several feet above the ground – people whose spiritual life was mysterious and heavenly. Such people should frequently experience visions and ecstatic revelations. They were the ones who deserved the honour and adulation of less worthy mortals whose ordinary lives were mundane and earthbound.

Paul felt nothing was to be gained by boasting of such experiences (12:1). But he felt he ought to demonstrate some important principles for the Corinthians, who were in danger of being captivated by the dramatic stories of spiritual exaltation, as if these were the essential elements of Christian life and leadership.

Indeed, Paul's reluctance to tell his own story is further underlined by his writing style. "I know a man," he says (v. 2), not wishing to be too up front about it. Such modesty is important for us to note in our world too, which shares with first-century Greek culture a sense of awe – even gullible superstition – when it comes to stories of remarkable visions.

1. A Heavenly Vision (12:1–6)

First, Paul's experience was so overwhelming that he was unable to describe it accurately. He was at a loss to find adequate words, and he could not easily fit the experience within his usual theological grid. Where did it take place? He wasn't sure (12:2–4). Was it in the body or out of the body? He didn't know (vv. 2–3). And what spiritual messages did he receive? He couldn't say (v. 4). Despite all of the uncertainties and qualifications, we can be sure that this was a profound moment, etched deeply on his memory. And we should never be cynical about the possibility of such an experience, for God has his purposes in the lives of those called to unique areas of ministry. While we are not told why Paul had such an experience, it was real enough.

Nevertheless, we should notice a second feature of the experience: it was highly unusual. Paul did not expect such experiences to be part of the normal Christian life. It had occurred fourteen years ago, and presumably Paul had no more recent examples to call on. So, while we should not be dismissive of such an experience, neither should we use this passage to argue that it should be a regular occurrence, or even expected for any other Christian.

He then underlines once again his reticence to speak about the experience (v. 5). We might have been tempted to secure a publisher or post an exciting video on social media. But Paul is reluctant to boast of anything save his weaknesses (v. 5). The experience he had described was real enough – it would not be foolish if he were to boast about it, for it was true (v. 6). His concern, however, was that he should be judged not on the basis of ecstatic experiences but on the basis of his words and actions (v. 6). It would be wise for us to take note. The people to learn from are not necessarily the ones with the dramatic stories or the spiritual "highs," but those whose words and actions demonstrate their commitment to serve the Lord Christ.

2. A Thorn in the Flesh (12:7–10)

Significantly, Paul's story of his spiritual experience doesn't end there. In contrast to his visit to paradise, he describes a very earthly problem. It is one of the best-known phrases of Paul: "I was given a thorn in my flesh" (12:7). The word used could also be translated "stake" or "splinter," and it is intended to convey an experience of some considerable pain.

There have been a range of ideas as to what this thorn represented. Was it some form of physical weakness – perhaps malaria, or epilepsy, or a speech impediment? Or was he referring to the opposition he encountered or the persecution inflicted on him by the Jews? One explanation is that it might relate to eye trouble. (He refers in Gal 4:13–15 to a bodily ailment, and indicates that the Galatians would have plucked out their eyes and given them to him; he then refers in Gal 6:11 to the large letters written in his own hand.) In fact, Paul does not tell us the exact cause of the painful affliction, and this has the particular benefit of making the text applicable to Christians through the centuries who have therefore been able to identify with its pain if not with its cause.

First, it was given to him for a special purpose: "to keep me from becoming conceited" (2 Cor 12:7). The remarkable spiritual experience which he has just described could have led to an ugly spiritual pride, and Paul is wise enough to interpret the thorn which had been inflicted on him as having the special benefit of pricking the balloon, of bringing down to size what might otherwise be an inflated ego. And whatever the cause of suffering in our lives, there is invariably such a positive purpose, if only we had the eyes to see it.

Further, he describes it as a messenger of Satan (v. 7). Paul frequently experienced Satanic resistance in his ministry, and he saw the thorn as part of Satan's harassment. But verse 7 implies that it achieved God's good purposes, and this is part of the Bible's teaching about Satanic activity. Satan acts only within the parameters which God sets (Job 2:6). So Paul can testify that even Satan's activity is overruled so that it achieves God's purpose. Once again, God's power is displayed in apparent weakness.

Notice, too, that Paul asked the Lord frequently to remove the thorn (v. 8). If weakness has no other purpose than to encourage us to turn to God in prayer, then it has performed a valuable function. All of us learn to pray best in suffering. It is also right for us to pray for healing. Paul has referred to the gift of healing in his first letter to the Corinthians, and James gives guidelines to church elders on the subject (Jas 5:13–18). But just as God has given us the encouragement to ask for healing, so there is a time to stop asking, and verse 8 implies that Paul received an unexpected answer to his prayer which became "the most powerful inspiration of his life."[1] (For further comment on this theme, see box labelled "Health and Wealth," p. 14.)

Significantly, Paul realized that God's purpose was not to bypass the difficulty but to transform it. Evil had lost the initiative. Now God's all-sufficient grace was poured into his life, not in spite of the thorn but *because* of that very weakness: "for [God's] power is made perfect in weakness" (2 Cor 12:9). Far from allowing his weakness to be an excuse for ducking out of demanding Christian service, it became the occasion for serving God with a new strength –

1. R. V. G. Tasker, *2 Corinthians*, Tyndale New Testament Commentaries (London: Tyndale Press, 1958), 178.

a strength not his own. God's grace was sufficient (the word implies "satisfied," and so goes further than "just enough" to include even a sense of comfort). Paul's breakthrough, as he wrote in chapter 4, was to understand that he was identified with Christ in his weakness and power.

Finally, Paul was therefore "well content" with weaknesses and would rather boast about these than about heroic exploits and great personal achievements. The super-apostles in Corinth would have had difficulty understanding it, but boasting about weaknesses was the radical difference between them and the apostle Paul. He was happy to declare his weakness – "gladly," "I will boast," "I delight" – because that was the time when Christ's power dwelt in him (v. 9). "For when I am weak, then I am strong" (v. 10).

Some Christians never feel such weakness because they never live their Christian lives beyond a cautiously safe limit. But those of us who feel our weaknesses and frailty, who identify in some measure with the insults, hardships, persecutions and difficulties to which Paul refers (v. 10), should take heart from these verses, and learn to turn to God for his super-abundant grace and resurrection power.

This is the central theme of the entire letter: weakness is the opportunity for the power of Christ to dwell in us. It will mean abiding in Christ, going to him, meditating upon him, understanding our union with him, living his life. As Paul was to write to the Philippians: "I want to know Christ – yes, to know the power of his resurrection and the participation in his sufferings" (Phil 3:10). So he could then conclude: "I can do all this through him who gives me strength" (Phil 4:13).

Questions

1. Repeated prayer requests for healing do not always result in the answer we are looking for. Why did this happen in Paul's case? What are the significant lessons? And what is the value of persistent prayer?

2. Paul knew there was something Satanic about the challenges he faced, but he also knew that God was in control and would bring about his good purposes. How would you help a fellow Christian, who felt themselves to be under spiritual attack, to gain this perspective of God's sovereign control?

3. Write a letter to a housebound and disabled friend, gently applying the central theme of 2 Corinthians that weakness is the opportunity for the power of Christ to dwell in us. In order to be pastorally sensitive, try to imagine what this person will feel on reading your letter.

4. Share examples with your group of how God's grace has proved sufficient for you through times of difficulty.

31

A True Apostle
2 Corinthians 12:11–19

> Serving the Lord means serving his people,
> and we must do so with steady perseverance
> and a deep concern for their well-being.

As Paul's extended self-defence draws to a close, two things have become clear. First, true spiritual ministry is not glamorous, nor does it display spectacular power or an impressive image. Rather, it steadily perseveres, experiences God's grace in weakness and utterly depends on his resources. Second, true spiritual ministry is fuelled not by a desire for personal gain or prestige but by a genuine commitment to serve others, to strengthen them in their Christian walk and to build up the church.

Both of these themes emerge in this section, as Paul concludes his defence. He has already referred to the "foolishness" of having to commend himself (11:1). He now repeats that he has been pushed to make a fool of himself because the Corinthians themselves have failed to stand up for him (12:11). He presents a series of arguments which represent his credentials as a true apostle, but through the section we will notice the twin themes to which we have referred – the contrast with the distorted image of "super-apostles" and Paul's clear motive of serving others.

1. Marks of a True Apostle (12:11–12)

In the eyes of the Corinthians he might be "nothing," but in fact he is "not in the least inferior to the 'super-apostles'" (12:11). In an intriguing phrase in verse 12, he explains his credentials.

First, one of the marks of his apostleship was to be found in the signs, wonders and miracles done among them (v. 12). Here Paul indicates that such evidences of God's power set the seal on the work of apostles. The book of Acts gives many examples of such signs and wonders, such as the healing of the lame man by Paul at Lystra (Acts 14:8–10) and the casting out of the evil spirit from the slave girl in Philippi (Acts 16:16–18). More seriously, we might add the death of Ananias and Sapphira in Acts 5 as equally an example of signs and wonders.

It is significant that Paul leaves this particular evidence of his apostleship until very late in his argument. Just as earlier in this chapter he has been reluctant to speak about ecstatic spiritual experiences (2 Cor 12:5–6), so now he does not play into the hands of those in Corinth for whom dramatic signs and wonders would have been the big headlines of their ministry. As we have seen throughout the letter, Paul would rather be judged by his faithfulness in living and proclaiming the gospel.

Second, Paul expresses himself carefully: "The signs of a true apostle were performed among you" (v. 12 ESV). He does not want to imply that they were to do with his special powers, but instead places the emphasis on the fact that God did such signs and wonders among them. Again, the understated way in which he presents his case is instructive to any Christian or church community which might be tempted to parade its spirituality inappropriately.

Third, Paul "persevered" in this ministry (v. 12). Perhaps this is the most direct clue to Paul's sense of priorities. His ministry was not one which offered the instant solution of the miraculous. Certainly, signs and wonders were in evidence, but his ministry was in the context of steady endurance, facing the pressures of serving Christ with a perseverance which, as this letter shows throughout, was to be the primary credential of ministry. Not the spectacular fireworks, not the super spiritual claims, but a life committed to serve the cause of Christ whatever the opposition and whatever the pressure.

2. Fatherly Care (12:13–19)

Behind the next few verses lie the criticisms of Paul that were associated with money: either that he had not requested payment for his work, which surely any "successful" leader would have done, or that he had manipulated the Corinthians and, through the collection (chs. 8 and 9), had exploited them, securing funds for personal gain under the guise of helping the needy in Jerusalem.

He replies with more than a hint of irony. "Forgive me for my failure to be a burden to you financially!" he implies (see 12:13; cf. 11:1–15). As he prepares for his third visit (12:14), he wants to assure them that his purpose is not to benefit financially from them. What he wants is their hearts, not their money. He longs for a restored relationship, a mutual commitment between the church and their spiritual father. Children are not expected to save up for their parents, he argues. So, in the same way, as the one who brought them to know Christ, his fatherly care for them means that he is interested not in financial gain but in their continued spiritual well-being. And he presses home the point in a moving phrase which could be applied to his apostolic ministry in all the churches: "So I will very gladly spend for you everything I have and expend myself as well" (v. 15).

He says much the same when writing to the Thessalonian Christians: "Because we loved you so much, we were delighted to share with you not only the gospel of God but our lives as well" (1 Thess 2:8). In the same passage he also uses the pictures of a mother who cares for her little children and a father who encourages, comforts and urges his children to live lives worthy of God (1 Thess 2:7; 2:11).

Paul is not arguing against the idea of payment for Christian ministry. Elsewhere he shows that it is right for a Christian minister to receive money (see 1 Cor 9:14; 1 Tim 5:17–18). But in Corinth he had deliberately avoided being a burden to the church and had shown his commitment to them by giving of himself fully and freely. It must have been very painful to be criticized for such sacrificial generosity.

Worse still, verses 16–18 of chapter 12 seem to imply that he was also being charged with deceitful behaviour by taking a cut from the Jerusalem offering. He appeals to them to remember the visit of the two brothers given the responsibility of taking up the offering. Just as they had not exploited the church, neither had he. We saw in chapters 8 and 9 how carefully the whole project had been administered, not least to avoid any appearance of exploitation or foul practice. "No," implies Paul, "we are not in the business of Christian ministry for personal gain, whether through the voluntary offerings of the church or through theft or deception." His ministry displays the selfless giving of a compassionate father towards his children.

The argument is given extra force in verse 19: "everything we do, dear friends, is for your strengthening." The past few chapters read like a sustained presentation of Paul's self-defence against the charges of his critics (v. 19). In reality, this has not been simply self-defence, but a reminder of Paul's apostolic authority which is essential for their own self-understanding, as we shall see in the next chapter. It is a serious business: he is "speaking in the sight of God" (v. 19). Paul's suffering has been for their benefit, not for personal gain. Even the struggles he faced, the criticisms he endured and the pressures of being associated with Christ: "everything we do, dear friends, is for your strengthening" (v. 19).

These are the marks of a true apostle. Not the exaggerated claims or financial interests of the super-apostles, but the steady endurance and selfless, compassionate care of a spiritual father. There are lessons here for all of us who are called to Christian ministry and leadership, for we face the temptations of money, power and influence too. The real test of genuine ministry will be the grace of perseverance and the gift of serving others.

Questions

1. Why are we sometimes tempted to think that Christian miracles are more important or more impressive than Christian character?

2. Paul describes his ministry towards others in 12:15: "I will very gladly spend for you everything I have and expend myself as well." Is that a mark of our service towards others in the church? What might it mean in practice if we lived like that?

3. Sometimes our Christian service is influenced by wrong motives – our desire for influence, power or money. Are there signs of this in our own lives? How can we avoid such traps?

32

Be Prepared

2 Corinthians 12:20–13:10

> With his third visit to Corinth now in view, Paul urges the believers to mend their ways if they are to avoid further apostolic discipline.

Paul has already referred to his upcoming third visit (12:14), and now he addresses his hopes and fears as he anticipates that time. In particular, this section will introduce some of the Corinthian failures, as well as Paul's determination to exercise his apostolic authority in church discipline if that is needed. So now he is writing to urge them to be prepared for his visit. He introduces clear warnings as he anticipates the need for discipline, knowing it will be painful for him and for them. There are important lessons here, because discipline is still a ministry to be exercised within the church today.

1. Why Discipline Is Needed (12:20–21)

We know from 1 Corinthians that many of the believers in the church were converted from pagan backgrounds, and that Paul had been concerned about the moral laxity in the church in the past (1 Cor 6:9–20). We know too that part of 2 Corinthians has been about previous moral failure (ch. 2). Now Paul writes with almost embarrassing frankness. He fears that when he arrives for his third visit, he will not find the Corinthian believers as mature in the faith as they should be, but guilty of all kinds of sin (12:20–21). In turn, this will mean that the Corinthians will not find Paul to be as they might have hoped.

Earlier in this letter Paul had defended himself against the charge that he was strong in his letters but weak when he met them. Now, he says, he will come among them with apostolic authority, ready to confront and discipline.

He lists some of the believers' community sins: "discord, jealousy, fits of rage, selfish ambition, slander, gossip, arrogance and disorder" (v. 20). These are ugly attitudes in the church, sadly still alive and well in our day. For they are Satan's chief weapons in the destruction of true Christian community, a community which should express the reconciling power of the gospel. Such sins not only discredit the church but effectively cast doubt on the transforming power of the gospel itself. No wonder Paul indicates that he will feel deep pain (v. 21) in confronting the believers and exercising discipline. Sexual sins, to which he refers in the next verse, are usually confronted in the church community today, but the failures in verse 20 are too often tolerated in our churches. They eat away at a church family, destroying it from within. Action is needed to root out the problem.

Then Paul refers to the sexual sins of some in the church and expresses grief at their failure to repent of "impurity, sexual sin and debauchery" (v. 21). The super-apostles appear to have ignored such behaviour, but Paul fires his volleys in advance of his visit. When he visits them, he will act decisively, and he turns to warn them of that possibility once again.

2. How Discipline Is Exercised (13:1–4)

Paul begins the final chapter with a quotation from Deuteronomy 19:15, expressing the legal requirement that two or three witnesses are needed to establish a case (2 Cor 13:1). We are not certain why Paul introduces this. It is likely that it is connected with his emphasis on his third visit: another visit will be adequate warning for them. He has already warned them on his second visit (13:2), calling them to repentance. He is now repeating that warning, and he will not be slow to act when he arrives (v. 2).

Jesus himself indicated the need for several witnesses (Matt 18:16), and in all church discipline we must be careful to ensure that there is adequate evidence and adequate warning. As we have already seen (2 Cor 12:20), rumour and gossip are sad features of church life, and every church leader needs to be careful to ensure that the facts are straight. Involvement of others in the ministry of church discipline is basic pastoral wisdom.

Paul describes how discipline will be exercised towards those who have not repented. He returns to the theme of weakness and power which has dominated the entire letter (13:3–4). The Corinthians had doubted Paul's authority as an apostle – Christ was not speaking through him, they thought. Now, he says, he will come with the authority of Christ. The pattern of Christ's weakness and power, of death and resurrection, is the pattern of all Christian ministry, as Paul has frequently explained. To be sure, Paul shares Christ's weakness. But they should not imagine this means he will not act authoritatively in dealing with sin within the church. Instead, "by God's power we will live with him in our dealing with you" (v. 4). He has the moral and spiritual authority to act in dealing with unrepentant church members. His union with Christ means both weakness in walking the pathway of suffering, and power and authority in the exercise of his ministry towards them.

3. How Discipline Can Be Avoided (13:5–10)

After such a sustained defence of his apostolic ministry, Paul appeals to the Corinthians, longing that they would respond. It is first and foremost an appeal for self-examination, urging them to test whether they genuinely belong to Christ (13:5). There are two reasons for this.

First, such an examination may lead them to see the reality of Christ's presence within them, and the need to live consistently in the light of it. Those who need to repent will do so; those who need to mature will press on to completeness (v. 9). Such self-examination is necessary as a spiritual check-up. By such regular, honest and prayerful check-ups, Christians will be able to avoid complacency and learn to grow in the faith in dependence on Christ. There would then be no need for the exercise of church discipline, for Christians will be disciplining their own lives.

Second, as the Corinthians discover the genuineness of their faith, they will in turn come to realize the genuineness of Paul's apostleship (v. 6). For their Christian faith is the result of his Christian ministry. If they are true believers, he must be a true apostle.

Paul then begins to draw the letter to a close by praying that they would move towards maturity – not doing anything wrong (v. 7) but doing what is right (v. 8) and experiencing the restoration and completeness which have been the underlying purpose of his ministry (v. 9). Again, in these closing sentences, Paul shows that his concern is for their well-being (vv. 7, 9). He has devoted himself to the truth, whatever his critics might say (v. 8), and his deepest concern is that his ministry will be to build them up (v. 10). As he anticipates his third visit, he longs that this should not be another "painful" one. He does not want to be harsh in his use of authority: he would much rather build up than tear down (v. 10).

Indeed, this has been the purpose of these tough chapters. Paul wants to shake them out of their self-satisfied complacency. He wants them to grow in grace. The whole purpose of his letter has been to exercise the authority the Lord gave him for building them up (v. 10). So straight talking has been a necessary part of that ministry, an expression of his love for them.

Discipline is never easy in a family, and certainly never easy in the church. But it is an essential part of healthy growth, and an expression of genuine love for one another.

Questions

1. Self-examination is an important element in personal spiritual growth. How can we ensure that it is not simply morbid and unhealthy introspection? What is healthy self-examination and what are its consequences?

2. Why are sins such as gossip, quarrelling, slander and arrogance so destructive to Christian community? Why do we treat them as less serious than, for example, sexual sins? How can we work to remove such attitudes from our own fellowship?

3. What place is there in the church today for discipline? How do you think it should be administered? What are the safeguards we need, especially when there is a danger of possible spiritual abuse?

33

Final Encouragements
2 Corinthians 13:11–14

> **Paul's closing advice comes in very significant bullet points and is supported by strong encouragement, reminding the Corinthians of God's provision of grace, love and fellowship.**

Most of us love movies and novels which have happy endings. Of course, too often that seems like Hollywood fantasy, for life doesn't always follow that script. But Paul's letter closes with some reasons to be cheerful. They are not trite Christian formulae or superficial greetings. They are specific encouragements to press forward.

Paul fires off his punchy exhortations as he closes his letter (verses 11–13):

Strive for full restoration. In 13:11 he repeats the prayer request of verse 9, using a word which really means "put in order." It comes from a word which is used in Mark's Gospel for mending nets. So, his call to the Corinthians and to us is this: mend your ways, make progress in your Christian life, restore your faith and commitment to Christ, get your act together. Don't be complacent about sin but be active in your dependence on God's grace. Aim for perfection!

Encourage one another. Respond to the truth of the gospel which the apostle has brought to you. Don't be distracted by the false values and ambitions of those around you but learn to live according to the pattern of Christ's death and resurrection, his power made perfect in weakness.

Be of one mind and live in peace. Display the true qualities of the redeemed and reconciled community. Live out the gospel of grace by the way you think and work together as God's people (v. 12). The commitment to be of one mind and to live in peace will have profound implications for all Christians, tempted as we are to echo the individualism and tribalism of our own societies and the selfishness of our own hearts.

Paul's final words point to how all of this is possible. First, he assures us of the protective love and peace of God (v. 11). The Spirit's ministry within the Corinthian church will be to make God's love and peace a reality. But second, the letter closes with words which have been spoken by the lips of Christians in every generation and in every culture (v. 14). They summarize Christian experience and are a fitting conclusion to a letter which, perhaps more than any other piece of human literature, has filled out the true meaning of God's grace. In trinitarian form, Paul expresses these good gifts:

- *The grace of the Lord Jesus Christ.* "You know the grace of our Lord Jesus Christ, that though he was rich, yet for your sakes he became poor, so that you through his poverty might become rich" (8:9). May this be your daily experience, Paul says, bringing to you all of God's riches and sufficiency for every situation in life (12:9).
- *The love of God.* He is the Father of compassion (1:3), who comforts you in all your troubles, whose love enfolds and surrounds you and from which you can never be separated.
- *The fellowship of the Holy Spirit.* The Spirit's presence is the characteristic feature of the new covenant ministry (3:6). His ministry is to guarantee our membership of God's family and our future inheritance (1:22; 5:5), to enable us to enjoy fellowship with God and to create a new community which reflects the reconciling power of the gospel.

When we say these words at the close of our church services, we remind one another that the whole of our Christian life and experience is focused around the Godhead. And that is where Paul wants to end this moving letter. Through the struggles of his life and work and the heartache of his relationship with the Corinthians, he returns to the solid foundations of the gospel – the Father who loves us, the Son who gave himself for us, the Spirit who now lives in us. That's the secret of being "strong in weakness" for Christians the world over.

Questions

1. What areas of our life need "mending" and restoring (13:11)? How can we embark on that process?

2. How can we turn the words of "the grace" (13:14) into a more meaningful prayer in our churches? Must it always come at the end of our prayers or services?

3. Think about each of the words Paul uses in his closing encouragements to the Corinthians – peace, love, grace and fellowship. What do each of these mean to us, and how can they make a deeper impact in our own lives and Christian community?

Langham
PARTNERSHIP

Langham Literature and its imprints are a ministry of Langham Partnership.

Langham Partnership is a global fellowship working in pursuit of the vision God entrusted to its founder John Stott –

to facilitate the growth of the church in maturity and Christ-likeness through raising the standards of biblical preaching and teaching.

Our vision is to see churches in the Majority World equipped for mission and growing to maturity in Christ through the ministry of pastors and leaders who believe, teach and live by the word of God.

Our mission is to strengthen the ministry of the word of God through:

- nurturing national movements for biblical preaching
- fostering the creation and distribution of evangelical literature
- enhancing evangelical theological education

especially in countries where churches are under-resourced.

Our ministry

Langham Preaching partners with national leaders to nurture indigenous biblical preaching movements for pastors and lay preachers all around the world. With the support of a team of trainers from many countries, a multi-level programme of seminars provides practical training, and is followed by a programme for training local facilitators. Local preachers' groups and national and regional networks ensure continuity and ongoing development, seeking to build vigorous movements committed to Bible exposition.

Langham Literature provides Majority World preachers, scholars and seminary libraries with evangelical books and electronic resources through publishing and distribution, grants and discounts. The programme also fosters the creation of indigenous evangelical books in many languages, through writer's grants, strengthening local evangelical publishing houses, and investment in major regional literature projects, such as one volume Bible commentaries like *The Africa Bible Commentary* and *The South Asia Bible Commentary*.

Langham Scholars provides financial support for evangelical doctoral students from the Majority World so that, when they return home, they may train pastors and other Christian leaders with sound, biblical and theological teaching. This programme equips those who equip others. Langham Scholars also works in partnership with Majority World seminaries in strengthening evangelical theological education. A growing number of Langham Scholars study in high quality doctoral programmes in the Majority World itself. As well as teaching the next generation of pastors, graduated Langham Scholars exercise significant influence through their writing and leadership.

To learn more about Langham Partnership and the work we do visit **langham.org**

Langham
PREACHING RESOURCES

By Jonathan Lamb

The Dynamics of Biblical Preaching
2016 | 9781907713774

Faith in the Face of Danger
An Introduction to the Book of Nehemiah
2018 | 9781783688913

From Why to Worship
An Introduction to the Book of Habakkuk
2018 | 9781783688920

Godliness from Head to Toe
An Introduction to the Book of James
2018 | 9781783688937

Also Available

Becoming Like Jesus
Cultivating the Fruit of the Spirit
Christopher J. H. Wright | 2016 | 9781783681068

The Challenge of Preaching
John Stott | 2011 | 9781907713118

Deuteronomy
The God Who Keeps Promises
Paul A. Barker | 2017 | 9781783681228

Echoes . . . The Lord's Prayer in the Preacher's Life
Geoff New | 2020 | 9781783688128

Focus on Christ
John Stott | 2019 | 9781783686209

The Future of Humanity
Preaching from Revelation 4 to 22
Murray Robertson | 2015 | 9781907713835

God's Word for Today's World
John Stott | 2015 | 9781783689378

It's OK to Be Not OK
Preaching the Lament Psalms
Federico G. Villanueva | 2017 | 9781907713989

Knowing Jesus through the Old Testament
Christopher J. H. Wright | 2014 | 9781907713996

Let the Gospels Preach the Gospel
Sermons around the Cross
Christopher J. H. Wright | 2017 | 9781783681426

Live, Listen, Tell
The Art of Preaching
Geoff New | 2017 | 9781783681624

Pastoral Preaching
Building a People for God
Conrad Mbewe | 2017 | 9781783681808

The Preacher's Portrait
Five New Testament Word Studies
John Stott | 2016 | 9781783680467

Reading the Gospel of John through Palestinian Eyes
Yohanna Katanacho | 2020 | 9781783687800

Relational Preaching
Knowing God, His Word, and Your Hearers
Greg Scharf | 2017 | 9781783682140

Sweeter than Honey
Preaching the Old Testament
Christopher J. H. Wright | 2015 | 9781783689347

What Angels Long to Read
Reading and Preaching the New Testament
Mark Meynell | 2017 | 9781783682669

What Christ Thinks of the Church
Preaching from Revelation 1 to 3
John Stott | 2019 | 9781783687022